Questions and Answe

Accounting

Questions & Answers

ACCOUNTING

Tony Hines
B.A. Econ (Hons)., P.G.C.E.

Checkmate/Arnold

First published in Great Britain 1986 by
Checkmate Publications,
4 Ainsdale Close, Bromborough, Wirral L63 0EU.

This edition published in association with

Edward Arnold (Publishers) Ltd.,
41 Bedford Square, London WC1B 3DQ

Edward Arnold (Australia) Pty Ltd.,
80 Waverley Road, Caulfield East,
Victoria 3145, Australia

Edward Arnold, 3 East Read Street,
Baltimore, Maryland 21202, USA.

ISBN 0 946973 27 7

Text set in 10/12pt Times by Merseyside Graphics Ltd.

Printed and bound by Richard Clay (The Chaucer Press),
Bungay, Suffolk

QUESTIONS AND ANSWERS IN ACCOUNTING

TABLE OF CONTENTS AND INDEX TO QUESTIONS AND ANSWERS

'So this is how you balance the books!'
(Graham Davies)

INTRODUCTION

The questions in this book have been chosen to give as wide a coverage of examination topics in Accounting as possible. Many of the questions are original and others are drawn from various examining bodies who have given their kind permission for questions to be reproduced. The following bodies have allowed their questions to be reproduced and I thank them for that:—

The Chartered Association of Certified Accountants (ACCA)
The Institute of Cost and Management Accountants (ICMA)
The Association of Accounting Technicians (AAT)

I must point out that these bodies have no responsibility for the solutions provided. The solutions are my responsibility and any errors therein.

The book is structured so that students may attempt questions in areas they are currently studying. Solutions may then be consulted to check answers. The book should prove useful to students for the following examinations:—

GCE 'O' and 'A' level Accounting
BTEC Accounting
Institute of Bankers
Institute of Chartered Secretaries and Administration
Institute of Cost and Management Accountants
The Chartered Association of Certified Accountants
The Association of Accounting Technicians
The Institute of Chartered Accountants Foundation

Tony Hines, January 1986

ACCOUNTANCY EXAMINATIONS AND YOU

1. BEFORE THE EXAM

You will be studying the subject matter of the examination. It is therefore essential that you are familiar with the syllabus for your examination. You should obtain a copy well in advance from the examining body.

You may be studying alone at home with recommended texts, following a correspondence course or receiving formal instruction at a college. It is harder to study at home and you need to approach the subject in a methodical manner by devising a work programme to ensure you cover topics on the syllabus within set times. Whatever your route of study the key to success is your ATTITUDE to study. You need to be DETERMINED to succeed. Success inevitably costs; it costs your time and effort. There are no 'free rides'. Look at it this way, why waste any time, money or effort on taking a course of study or in suffering in an examination in which you stand no chance or little chance of success. Therefore, if you are going to spend time, effort and money, put yourself in with a good chance of success by attacking the problem in a systematic and determined way.

REGULAR study in a SYSTEMATIC way is essential to your success, more so, in accounting than other subjects which you may think you can 'CRAM' for, although I would not recommend that either.

During your course, you should:—

1 PLAN your study time each week

2 SET the work you want to cover

3 ALLOW extra time to revise topics previously studied, so as they 'stick'.

4 HAVE all the tools to hand — Notes, texts, calculators, pens, pencils, rulers etc.

5   ENVIRONMENT — a comfortable, quiet room with no distractions from the job at hand is essential, where you will not be interrupted.

6   DO NOT WASTE time. It is a valuable commodity and a finite one. Start work immediately — Do not decide to read a paper, doodle, watch T.V. or whatever, during your study time. You should be strict with yourself on this issue.

7   PRESENT any work you do in a neat manner, pay attention to detail. Students often present work to me which is untidy and would be unacceptable in an examination. The reasons (excuses) I receive vary from — ''I did it quickly'' — ''It's only rough'' — ''I wanted to see it was right before I wrote it in ink'' etc. You should get into the habit of writing your answers neatly and in ink — not pencil. Your speed will improve and you will be in shape to take the exam. Pencils are not usually accepted in examination scrips; therefore, **do not** get into the habit of using them. Just like joggers are attempting to fine tune their bodies for fitness, you are getting your examination technique into shape.

8   Where you are following a formal course of study, ensure that you take good notes that are good enough to jog your memory about important points. Rewrite them when you get home, if necessary. Always read them and practise any questions or techniques set.

9   Organize your file into topic areas in line with the syllabus you are studying. Any questions you do on each topic should be at the end of your notes on the topic, so as not to 'mess' up the text.

10   Take notice of the weightings given to each topic when allocating your study time. For example, if 5% of the syllabus is devoted to Depreciation, then it might be an idea to allocate 5% of your total study time to that topic. However, you should not be too rigid, since it takes different people different amounts of time to grasp a particular topic. The message is not to spend an inordinate amount of time on any single item.

11 FINAL EXAM — You should prepare for this by obtaining past questions and doing as many of those questions as possible without reference to notes. This book should have helped you in your approach to questions. I would recommend you to obtain at least 4 to 6 past papers. You should, however, ensure that the examination papers set in the past are going to be similar to the one you are taking. OR HAVE THERE BEEN SYLLABUS CHANGES?

11.1 Attempt at least one complete paper under examination conditions. Answer questions correctly, neatly and in the time.

11.2 Study your answers and see where and why you went wrong, noting improvements you could make.

2. DURING THE EXAM

1 Ensure you arrive in plenty of time.

2 Do not try reading notes immediately before the exam, they will only confuse you. If you don't know it now, it's too late for this one.

3 Ensure you have the necessary tools with you to do a good job (pen, pencil, rubber, ruler, calculator etc.)

4 Ensure you have your examination reference number and identification.

5 When you receive the paper, read the instructions carefully. Note how many questions you need to answer.

6 READ quickly through all the questions, marking those you think you can best answer. Ask yourself the following:— How many questions do I need to answer? Are any questions compulsory? How many marks are allocated to each question and each section of the question?

7   Allocate your time in proportion to the possible marks you can earn. Remember, in a three hour exam you could earn a possible 100%, therefore, each percentage point should be earned in no more than 1.8 minutes, i.e. $\frac{180 \text{ minutes}}{100\%}$ A question worth 20 marks should therefore have a time allowance of 36 minutes (20 x 1.8). This planning is essential to the most effective use of your time and should take no longer than 5 minutes.

8   Do not waste time. Remember if you score half marks on all the required questions, you will pass the examination. It is essential you do not spend time inefficiently trying to squeeze an extra 10% from a question by spending a further 20 minutes over and above the allowed time for that question.

9   Make sure you answer the question the examiner set and cover the relevant points.

10   Attempt all the questions you need to. If the paper asks you to complete five questions all worth 20 marks each — DO FIVE. If you only do four, you immediately write off 20 possible marks. Therefore, ensure you keep an eye on the time and answer all the questions you need to.

3.   AFTER THE EXAM

Forget about it unless you're into unnecessary pain and self torture. Post mortems at this stage do not achieve anything.

Finally, GOOD LUCK!

QUESTION 1

ACCOUNTING PRINCIPLES AND PRACTICE

The accounts of a small business have recently come into your possession and are reproduced below.

M. and A. Margan
Trading and profit and loss account
for year ended 30 April 1985

	£	£
Sales — cash	72,010	
— credit	83,206	
		155,216
Less		
Opening stock	18,352	
Purchases	124,693	
	143,045	
Closing stock	(21,824)	
Goods used by owner	(640)	
Cost of sales		120,581
Gross profit		34,635
Add		
Trade discounts received on purchases	16,530	
Value added tax included in purchases	14,500	
		31,030
		65,665
Less		
Wages and salaries	28,726	
Value added tax included in sales	16,000	
Goods used by owner	640	
Heating and lighting	6,127	
Depreciation	5,760	
Other expenses	4,036	
		61,289
Net profit for year		£4,376

M. and A. Margan
Balance sheet as at 30 April 1985

	£	£
Fixed assets		
Premises	44,000	
Vehicles	10,240	
		54,240
Current assets		
Stock	21,824	
Debtors	6,017	
Bank and cash	511	
	28,352	
Current liabilities		
Creditors	27,809	
		543
		54,783
Capital: opening	53,000	
: net profit for year	4,376	
	57,376	
: drawings	(6,000)	
		51,376
Unidentified difference in books		3,407
		54,783

Explanatory notes:

Sales

The figure shown comprises amounts actually received, (including value added tax) for both cash and credit sales after deducting cash discounts for prompt settlement of accounts. The value added tax element is then charged as an expense.

Cost of sales

Opening stock has been valued at FIFO (first in, first out) purchase cost but during the year it has been thought appropriate to take account of storage and handling charges; consequently closing stock includes a surcharge of 5% to cover this item.

Purchases are included at gross catalogue price (including value added tax). Both reclaimable value added tax and trade discounts on purchases are then shown as additional items of revenue.

Wages and salaries
This item comprises the amounts actually paid within the year, irrespective of the period in which they were earned.

Depreciation
Premises have been depreciated on a straight line basis on cost, assuming a 50 year life.

Vehicles have been depreciated at the rate of 20% per annum on a reducing balance basis.

Required:
Identify and comment upon the specific instances in which the accounts of the business have been prepared in apparent conflict with generally accepted accounting principles, practices and conventions. *(16 marks)*

(ACCA)

QUESTION 2

After stocktaking for the year ended 31 May 1985 had taken place, the closing stock of Cobden Ltd. was aggregated to a figure of £87,612.

During the course of the audit which followed, the undernoted facts were discovered:

(1) Some goods stored outside had been included at their normal cost price of £570. They had, however, deteriorated and would require an estimated £120 to be spent to restore them to their original condition, after which they could be sold for £800.

(2) Some goods had been damaged and were now unsaleable. They could, however, be sold for £110 as spares after repairs estimated at £40 had been carried out. They had originally cost £200.

(3) One stock sheet had been over-added by £126 and another under-added by £72.

(4) Cobden Ltd. had received goods costing £2,010 during the last week of May 1985 but because the invoices did not arrive until June 1985, they have not been included in stock.

(5) A stock sheet total of £1,234 had been transferred to the summary sheet as £1,243.

(6) Invoices totalling £638 arrived during the last week of May 1985 (and were included in purchases and in creditors) but, because of transport delays, the goods did not arrive until late June 1985 and were not included in closing stock.

(7) Portable generators on hire from another company at a charge of £347 were included, at this figure, in stock.

(8) Free samples sent to Cobden Ltd. by various suppliers had been included in stock at the catalogue price of £63.

(9) Goods costing £418 sent to customers on a sale or return basis had been included in stock by Cobden Ltd. at their selling price, £602.

(10) Goods sent on a sale or return basis to Cobden Ltd. had been included in stock at the amount payable (£267) if retained. No decision to retain had been made.

Required:

Using such of the above information as is relevant, prepare a schedule amending the stock figure as at 31 May 1985. State your reason for each amendment or for not making an amendment. *(16 marks)*

(ACCA)

QUESTION 3

'Financial reports should be completely objective. Subjective judgements have no place in accounting.' Discuss.

(15 marks)

(ICMA)

QUESTION 4 — Capital and Revenue

1. The estimated net profit for Dalglish Limited for the year ended 31st March 1985 is £10,100 before the following items are taken account of:

(a) The cost of a new workshop built during the year and completed on 30th September 1984 at a cost of £20,000.

(b) The cost of a new word processor bought on 1st January 1985 for £2,500.

(c) Repairs to typewriters incurred on 1st January 1985 — £500.

(d) The cost of installing a re-conditioned engine in a delivery van on 30th June 1984 — £500.

(e) Legal expenses paid in respect of the new workshop — £500.

It is the policy of Dalglish Ltd. to charge depreciation as follows:—

(i) Buildings are written off in equal instalments over 20 years.

(ii) All plant, machinery and office equipment is written off over 10 years on a straight line basis.

(iii) Motor vehicles are written off at 25% p.a. on a reducing balance basis.

N.B. Depreciation is apportioned on a monthly basis.

Required:

1.(a) Distinguish between Capital and Revenue Expenditure.

(b) Explain with reference to each of the items (a) to (e) above why you have chosen to classify each of them either as Capital or Revenue Expenditure.

2. Calculate a revised estimated profit after taking account of each of the items (a) to (e) and show your answer clearly in the form of a statement.

(20 marks)

QUESTION 5

Johnny Whizkid runs his own business trading in second hand motor cars. He calls into the bank to see you to obtain some advice. He says he understands what cash is but he cannot understand all the 'mumbo jumbo' his accountant talks about — Profit and Loss Statements, Balance Sheets and so on. He says that the bank must know about these things and since they have always been so helpful in the past at translating jargon into plain English could they do so now. He would particularly like to know what the accountant means when he says the following:—

1. Profit is not cash.
2. Depreciation is not cash.
3. The value of the business is not necessarily the Balance Sheet total.
4. Liquidity is important for short term survival but profitability is equally important in the longer term.
5. Financial statements need to be consistent, prudent and drawn up on the going concern basis to be meaningful to users.

Required:
Write notes for Mr. Whizkid, setting out in as easily understood a manner as possible, what the accountant means when he makes each of the above statements. *(20 marks)*

QUESTION 6

Company financial statements, including profit and loss accounts, balance sheets and statements of source and application of funds, are used by a variety of individuals and institutions for a wide variety of purposes.

Required:
Specify six different types of users of financial statements and explain in each case the aspects of performance or position in which they are interested. *(16 marks)*

(ACCA)

QUESTION 7

JOHNNY BARROW — Trial Balance at 31.12.84

	£Dr	£Cr
FIXED ASSETS		
Motor Vehicle	15,000	
Machinery	12,000	
Land & Buildings	50,000	
CURRENT ASSETS		
Stock	7,500	
Debtors	6,250	
Bank	1,250	
Cash	500	
PURCHASES	25,000	
EXPENSES		
Secretarial	1,500	
Wages	3,000	
Advertising	2,100	
Bad Debts	150	
Discount Allowed	50	
DRAWINGS	1,500	
CREDITORS		5,250
CAPITAL		50,000
SALES		35,500
LOAN — VAN HIRE		400
PROVISION		
Bad Debts		50
Depreciation Motor Vehicles		6,000
Machinery		3,600
Land and Buildings		25,000
	£125,800	£125,800

1) Stock 31.12.84 — £5,350
2) Provision for Bad Debts should be made equivalent to 2% of closing Debtor balance.

3) Advertising expenditure incurred but not yet invoiced £250.
4) £100 secretarial expenses are in respect of January 1985.
5) Depreciation policy is as follows:—
   Motor Vehicles   = 20% p.a. Straight Line
   Machinery   = 10% p.a. Reducing Balance
   Land & Buildings = written off over 50 years equally

Required:
1) A working paper showing adjustments.
2) A Trading and Profit & Loss Account for the year ended 31.12.84.
3) A Balance Sheet at 31.12.1984.   *(20 marks)*

QUESTION 8

Fred's Trial Balance at 30.6.84

	£Dr	£Cr
Premises	10,000	
Motor vehicle	5,500	
Machinery	3,500	
Debtors	4,100	
Stock 1.7.83	3,250	
Cash	600	
Advertising	250	
Rent	100	
Rates	150	
Administration	600	
Distribution	120	
Creditors		3,320
Capital		20,000
Loan		5,000
Purchases	10,150	
Sales		10,000
	£38,320	£38,320

Notes:
(1) Stock at 30.6.84 £5,000.
(2) Rates for 12 months to 30.6.84 payable at £10 per month.
(3) In addition to advertising expenses shown in Trial Balance £30 is due to local newspaper.

(4) It is expected that further delivery charges will be made against distribution costs amounting to £50.

Required
1. A working paper showing the necessary adjustments.
2. A Trading and Profit and Loss Account for the year to 30.6.1984.
3. A Balance Sheet at 30.6.1984.

(15 marks)

QUESTION 9

H. LAMAR — Trial Balance at 31.12.84

	£DR	£CR
FIXED ASSETS:		
Land & buildings	50,000	
Motor vehicle	15,000	
CURRENT ASSETS:		
Stock at 1.1	7,500	
Debtors	6,250	
Bank	2,500	
Cash	300	
PURCHASES	21,500	
EXPENSES:		
Advertising	2,500	
Rent	2,600	
Light & heat	550	
M.V. running	1,120	
Accommodation	250	
Bad debts	100	
DRAWINGS	1,000	
CREDITORS		5,500
CAPITAL		50,000
LOAN from Mayor		4,570
SALES		30,000
PROVISION for bad debts		200
PROVISIONS for Depreciation		
Land and Buildings		15,000
Motor Vehicle		5,400
RETURNS inwards	500	
RETURNS outwards		1,000
	£111,670	£111,670

Notes:
1) Stock 31.12.84 £4,750.
2) A credit sale made on 31.12.84 £1,000 has been completely omitted from the books.
3) A provision for bad debts should be made equivalent to 5% of closing debtor balance.

4) No expense has been included for interest on loan which was paid by cheque on 31.12.84. Interest is 10% of capital sum. No adjustment has been made to the bank account.
5) Rent is payable at £200 per month.
6) Accommodation expenses incurred but not yet invoiced or paid amount to £150.
7) Depreciation is to be provided as follows:
   1) Land and Buildings are written off over useful life by equal instalments; estimated life 50 years.
   2) Motor Vehicles are written off at 20% p.a. on reducing balance basis.

Required:
1) A working paper showing necessary adjustments.
2) A trading and profit and loss account for year end 31.12.84.
3) Balance sheet as at 31.12.84.

(20 marks)

QUESTION 10

Rod commences in business exporting wine. He begins with £6,000 of his own money and £3,000 that he borrows from his friend.

He buys premises for £4,000 cash and he buys a delivery van for £2,000 cash.

He buys stock for resale £3,000 on credit terms.

He incurs the following expenses: buying trips £750 cash; entertaining clients £150 on credit terms; advertising £50 credit.

He sells stock for £2,500 to debtors.

At the close of the 3 month period to the 31st March 1984 his stock was valued at cost price per the stock take, £1,150.

Required

1. The individual accounts necessary to record the above transactions.
2. Construct a Trial Balance at the 31st March 1984.
3. A Trading and Profit and Loss Account for the 3 months.
4. A Balance Sheet as at 31st March 1984.

5. Estimate his gross profit as a percentage sales, i.e. the Gross Margin.

(20 marks)

QUESTION 11

MICKY — Trial Balance at 31.12.85

	£ Dr	£ Cr
Land & Buildings a cost	100,000	
Motor Vehicles a cost	10,000	
Plant & Machinery a cost	25,000	
Stock 1-1-85	4,750	
Debtors	5,250	
Bank	3,200	
Cash	1,000	
Purchases	22,000	
Carriage Inwards	150	
Carriage Outwards	200	
Returns Inwards	250	
Returns Outwards		500
Drawings	4,100	
Discount allowed	450	
Discount received		700
Wages & Salaries	5,100	
Advertising	2,200	
Travelling	1,000	
Accommodation	500	
Rent	900	
Rates	300	
Postage & Stationery	150	
Light & heat	2,250	
Provision for Depreciation:—		
Land & Buildings (L & B)		40,000
Plant & Machinery (P & M)		4,750
Motor Vehicles (MV)		4,000
Sales		50,000
Creditors		4,800
Capital		80,000
Loan (long term liability)		4,000
	188,750	188,750

Notes:
1. Stock 31-12-85 £4,750.
2. Depreciation is to be charged
    L & B 2% per annum on cost
    P & M 10% per annum reducing balance
    MV 20% per annum on cost
    The rent expense shown in the Trial Balance is in respect of
    the period from the 1.1.85 to the 30.9.85.
4. Rate expenses shown in the Trial Balance are in respect of
    the period 1.1.85 — 31.3.85. The rating year runs from the
    1.4.85 — 31.3.86. Rates for 85/86 have increased by 10%
    over the previous year's figure.
5. Within the expense account, postage & stationery is the
    cost of replenishing the franking machine. At the close on
    the 31.12.85 the meter on this machine showed £49 still
    available for use.

Required:
You are required to:
1. Prepare a Trading and Profit & Loss A/c for the year ending
    31.12.85.
2. Prepare a Balance Sheet as at 31.12.85.

(20 marks)

QUESTION 12

The following was a receipts and payments account prepared by the treasurer of the Mid-Cheshire Cricket Club for the year ended 31 December 1984.

1984	RECEIPTS	£Dr	1984	PAYMENTS	£Cr
1.1	Cash in hand	20	31.12	Groundsman's fees	150
	Balances at bank as per bank statements:			Purchase of mowing machine	300
	Deposit a/c	446		Rent of ground	50
	Current a/c	120		Cost of teas	50
31.12	Bank interest on deposit account	6		Fares	80
	Donations and subscriptions	520		Printing and secretarial exp.	56
	Receipts from teas	60		Repairs to equipment and machinery	100
	Contributions to fares	20		Honoraria to secretary and treasurer for 1983	40
	Sale of equipment	16		Balances at bank as per bank statements:	
	Net proceeds of dance	156		Deposit a/c	418
				Current a/c	30
				Cash in hand	50
		1,364			1,364

You are given the following additional information:

		On 1 Jan. 1984 £	On 31 Dec. 1984 £
(1)	Subscriptions due	30	20
(2)	Sums due for printing and secretarial expenses	20	16
(3)	Unpresented cheques, being payments for repairs	60	50

(4) Interest on deposit accounts
not yet credited on bank
statements   —   4

(5) Estimated value of
machinery and equipment   160   350

(6) For the year ended 31 December
1984 the honoraria to the
secretary and treasurer are to
be increased by a total of £20
and the groundsman is to receive
a bonus of £20.

Required:
You are required to prepare:
(a) a computation showing the capital of the club on
1 January 1984;   *(5 marks)*
(b) an income and expenditure account for the year ended
31 December 1984; and   *(10 marks)*
(c) a balance sheet on that date.   *(5 marks)*

QUESTION 13
The treasurer of the WIRRAL CRICKET CLUB has prepared
the receipts and payments account shown below. He would like
to prepare a more appropriate financial statement and asks you
as a friend if you could assist him.

Required:
1. Advise the treasurer what type of account you consider
   more appropriate and why.
2. Prepare the financial statement to illustrate your answer to
   1 above. Show all workings.   *(20 marks)*

WCC Receipts and Payments Account for the year ended 31.12.83

	RECEIPTS	£Dr		PAYMENTS	£Cr
1.1.83	Bank balance b/f	1,048		Bar supplies	7,924
				Wages:	
	Subscriptions	2,662		Groundsman	1,878
	Bar Sales	11,256		Barman	1,248
	Donations	240		Bar Expenses	468
				Repairs to	
				Clubhouse	238
				Ground upkeep	458
				Secretary Exp.	276
				Coach Hire	610
			31.12.83	Bank balance c/f	2,106
		15,206			15,206

The treasurer also provides the following information:

		31.12.82 £	31.12.83 £
1.	Bar stock at cost	992	1116
	Owing for bar supplies	588	680
	Bar Expenses owing	50	70
	Coach hire owing	—	65
	Subscriptions due	110	132

2. £80 subscriptions have been received in advance during 1983.
3. The land was valued at 31.12.82 at £8,000 and the Clubhouse at £4,000. The latter is to be depreciated at 10% p.a.
4. Equipment was valued at 31.12.82 at £1,100 and is to be depreciated at 20% p.a.

QUESTION 14

Using the information given below, which relates to a manufacturing company Jones Limited, you are required to prepare a statement to show clearly:—   *(20 marks)*

(a) Cost of raw materials consumed
(b) Prime cost
(c) Cost of finished goods produced
(d) Cost of finished goods sold
(e) Gross Profit
(f) Net Profit

for the year ended 30 April 1982.

		£
Raw Materials:	Stock at 1 May 1981	45,000
	Purchases	154,000
	Stock at 30 April 1982	49,000
Finished Goods:	Stock at 1 May 1981	60,000
	Purchases	11,000
	Stock at 30 April 1982	68,000
Work-in-progress	at 1 May 1981	21,000
	at 30 April 1982	23,200
Sales		500,000
Manufacturing Wages		80,000
Manufacturing Expenses		30,300
Repairs & Maintenance of Plant & Machinery		18,500
Depreciation:	Factory	40,000
	General Office	8,000
	Sales Warehouse	9,000
Carriage outwards		6,600
Power		15,000
Light and Heat:	Factory	5,400
	General Office	800
	Sales Warehouse	3,300
Administration expenses		22,200
Selling and distribution expenses		31,100

QUESTION 15

Summers Ltd. carries on a business as a manufacturer, the trial balance extracted from the books at 31st March '84 is as follows:—

	DR	CR
Drawings	1,600	
Light & heat Office	138	
Factory	1,445	
Manufacturing wages	10,054	
Office Salaries	2,116	
Advertising	808	
Stock Raw Materials (@1.4.83)	7,102	
WIP (@1.4.83)	3,500	
Finished Goods (@1.4.83)	7,278	
Sundry Expenses Office	399	
Factory	530	
Purchase of Raw Materials	49,944	
Salesman's Commission	880	
Premises at cost	4,050	
Plant (Cost 10,000)	7,500	
Trade Debtors	7,575	
Cash & Bank	2,013	
Office Machinery (Cost 1,000)	500	
Rent & Rates Office	69	
Factory	150	
Capital A/C		22,650
Bank Loan		5,600
Trade Creditors		7,733
Sales		71,580
	107,563	107,563

Notes:
1. A provision for bad debts is to be made equal to 4% of trade debtors.
2. Stocks at 31.3.84 Raw Material 7,064
   WIP 2,500
   Finished goods 7,448
3. Depreciation is to be provided on plant 5% per annum on cost.
4. Office machinery valued at £400 on 31.3.84.
5. Wages unpaid at 31.3.84 £136. Advertising prepaid £48.

You are required to:
(a) Prepare a Manufacturing and Trading and Profit and Loss Account for the year ended 31st March 1984.
(b) Prepare a Balance Sheet for Summers Ltd. as at 31st March 1984.

(20 marks)

QUESTION 16
Dalglish and Rush were in partnership sharing profits in the ratio of 3:2 i.e. 3/5 to Dalglish and 2/5 to Rush. The following is a list of balances extracted from their books at 31.12.83.

	£Dr	£Cr
Capital at 1.1.83		
Dalglish		10,000
Rush		6,000
Current A/c at 1.1.83		
Dalglish		2,000
Rush		1,000
Drawings:		
Dalglish	3,000	
Rush	2,500	
Premises	4,000	
Fixtures	2,000	
Stock at 1.1.83	2,500	
Bad debts	200	
Purchases	16,000	
Sales		24,000
Debtors	6,000	
Creditors		3,000
Cash	800	
Wages	4,000	
Advertising	3,000	
Insurance	1,000	
Sundry Expenses	500	
Returns In	200	
Discount Allowed	300	
	46,000	46,000

Notes:
1. Stock on 31.12.1983 — £2,800.
2. Depreciation is charged as follows:—
   Premises 10% per annum straight line basis
   Fixtures 20% per annum straight line basis.
3. Interest is to be paid at 5% per annum on the partners' Capital accounts.
4. Wages accrued £500.
5. Provision for bad debts is to be made 2.5% on sales shown in the Trading and Profit and Loss Account.

Required
1. Prepare a trading, profit and loss, appropriation account and partners' current accounts for the year ended 31.12.83.
2. A Balance Sheet at 31.12.83.
3. Briefly explain the accounting steps to be followed in dissolving the partnership should it become necessary.

(30 marks)

QUESTION 17 — Partnership

DUM & DEE — Trial Balance at 31.12.85

	£Dr	£Cr
Fixed Assets:		
Land and Buildings a cost	100,000	
Motor Vehicle a cost	20,000	
Current Assets:		
Stock a 1.1.85	5,550	
Debtors	7,250	
Bank	3,200	
Cash	510	
Purchases	29,525	
Carriage inwards	100	
Discount received	300	
Expenses:		
Administration:		
Wages & Salaries	7,500	
Office Repairs	500	
Telephones	350	
Rent & Rates of Office	1,800	
Sales & Marketing:		
Advertising	2,750	
Salesman's Salary	8,000	
Vehicle Running	2,150	
Discount Allowed	1,000	
Distribution:		
Vehicle Running	4,250	
Vehicle Repairs	1,100	
Carriage Outwards	1,000	
Finance: Bank Charges	550	
Sales		51,550
Creditors		7,650
Provision for Depreciation:		
Land & Buildings		30,000
Motor Vehicle		5,000
Partners Capital Accounts:		
Dum		50,000
Dee		40,000
Partners Current Accounts:		
Dum		8,185
Dee		4,400
	197,085	197,085

Notes:
1. Stock valued at cost 31.12.85 was £5,385.
2. It is policy to charge depreciation as follows:—
    (a) Land & Buildings are to be written off in equal instalments over the estimated useful life which the partners deem to be 50 years.
    (b) Motor Vehicles are written off at 20% p.a. at cost. (75% of the vehicles are used for distribution purposes, the remainder are used as sales vehicles).
3. The partners have agreed to pay interest on fixed capitals at 5% p.a. They have also agreed to charge interest on drawings at 10% p.a.
4. Dee receives a salary of £5,000 p.a. in respect of extra duties he undertakes.
5. The partners have agreed to share Profits & Losses equally.
6. Drawings paid by cheque during the year, not included in the Trial Balance were as follows:—

	£
Dum	1,200
Dee	500

The money having been withdrawn from the bank no entries have been made into the accounts as yet.
7. The Rent & Rates charge of £1,800 is in respect of the period from 1 January 1985 to 30 June 1986.
8. Further advertising expenses amounting to £750 were incurred. No invoice having yet been received and no cash having been paid.

Required:
1. Prepare a partnership Trading, Profit & Loss and Appropriation A/c for the year ended 31.12.85.
2. Show the partners' Capital & Current Account at 31.12.85.
3. Draw up a Balance Sheet for the partnership as at 31.12.85.   *(25 marks)*

QUESTION 18

A record business, Hot Rod Records, had grown from strength to strength and in early 1984 the partners decided to sell the business to one of their competitors. The balance sheet showed the following position, the partners sharing profits equally:

Hot Rod Records Balance Sheet at 30.6.1984

Fixed assets	£Cost	£Depn.	£NBV
Lease	20,000	6,000	14,000
Fixtures and fittings	3,000	1,800	1,200
Motor van	1,600	500	1,100
	24,600	8,300	16,300

Current assets		
Stock	17,000	
Debtors	15,200	
Bank	6,400	
	38,600	

Current liabilities		
Creditors	7,800	
Net Current Assets (Working Capital)		30,800
Total Net Assets		47,100

Capital Accounts	£	£
Keith		12,000
Tony		8,000
Neil		6,000
Geoff		4,000
		30,000

Current Accounts		
Keith	4,160	
Tony	4,920	
Neil	4,240	
Geoff	3,780	
		17,100
		47,100

The following assets were sold for cash:

	£
Lease	18,000
Fixtures and fittings	800
Stock	16,400
Debtors	15,000
Goodwill	24,000
TOTAL PROCEEDS	74,200

The motor van was taken over by Neil at a valuation of £1,260. The creditors were paid in full and the bank account was closed.

Required:

1. The realisation account. *(8 marks)*
2. The closing Cash Book. *(4 marks)*
3. Partners' Current Accounts after realisation. *(4 marks)*
4. Partners' Capital Accounts after realisation. *(4 marks)*

QUESTION 19

The following information is available concerning Lewis's Sales Ledger Control Account:—

	£
Debtors 1.1.1984	7,504
Returns inwards	812
Cheques dishonoured	50
Credit sales in year to 31.12.84	49,836
Cheques from debtors	42,074
Cash from debtors	1,122
Purchase ledger contra	252
Bad debt written off	86
Bad debt provision 31.12.84	254
Cash sales	6,018

(a) From the information above you are required to write up the Sales Ledger Control Account for the year ended 31 December 1984. *(10 marks)*

Lewis extracts his list of debtors' balances at 31 December 1984 and they total £13,294.

He discovers:
1. £60 received from Evans whose debt of £600 had been written off in 1984 had been credited to the control account. Since no ledger card existed for him, the receipt was not entered in the Sales ledger. Evans has recently died penniless.
2. The sales day book has been undercast by £200.
3. A contra with the purchase ledger of £40 with the accounts of Going has not been entered in the control account.
4. The account of Newton which shows a credit balance of £130 has been shown as a debit balance in the list of balances.
5. Lamb's account with a debit balance of £160 has been omitted from the list of balances.
6. Discounts of £70 recorded in the sales ledger were not shown in the Sales Ledger Control Account.

(b) You are required to show the necessary adjustments to the Sales Ledger Control Account (starting with the balance calculated in part **(a)** and **(c)** to prepare a statement reconciling the list of balances with the balance on the Sales Ledger Control Account. *(6 marks)*

QUESTION 20

(a) From the following information you are required to prepare a Sales Ledger Control Account for the month of May 1984 for T. Ltd.

		£
May 1	Sales Ledger — debit balances	7,632
May 1	Sales Ledger — credit balances	44
May 31	Transactions for the month	
	Cash received	208
	Cheques received	12,478
	Sales	14,180
	Bad debts written off	612
	Discounts allowed	596
	Returns inwards	328
	Cash refunded to a customer who has	
	overpaid his account	74
	Dishonoured cheques	58

The list of balances at the month end were:—

	£
Sales Ledger — debit balances	7,758
Sales Ledger — credit balances	80

(b) Briefly explain the purpose of control accounts.

(16 marks)

QUESTION 21

Certain balances in a company's ledger at 30th June, 1980 were:

	£
Debtors	20,000
Provision for bad debts	1,000
Stock of coke.........	630
Electricity accrued	920

During the year to 30th June, 1981 the following transactions occurred:

	£
Sales on credit...................................	200,000
Cash received from debtors	193,000
Certain debtors became bankrupt, and their debts were written off against the provision	3,000
Certain debts which had been written off as bad in previous years were recovered in cash and transferred to the provision	1,000
Purchases of coke...............................	8,000
Payments for electricity for the year ended 30th April, 1981	6,000

At 30th June, 1981 the stock of coke was valued at £750, and the provision for bad debts was adjusted to be equal to 5% of the debtors. On 6th August, 1981 the company paid its electricity account of £1,010 for the quarter ended 31st July, 1981.

Required:

You are required to show the debtors, provision for bad debts and lighting and heating accounts in the company's ledger for the year ended 30th June, 1981.   *(15 marks)*

(ICMA)

QUESTION 22

From the following information supplied by Zee Ltd. you are required to prepare a Creditors Control Account showing the balance to carry forward at 31.1.1986.

		£
January 1st	Purchase Ledger Balance b/f	105,650
During January	Purchase Journals	115,675
	Returns Outward	7,860
	Discount Received	10,850
	Payments by Cheque to Creditors	104,650
	Payments to Creditors by Cash	1,000

(10 marks)

QUESTION 23

D. HOFFMAN — Trial Balance at 31.12.84

	£Dr	£Cr
Fixed Assets		
L & B	100,000	
Machinery	50,000	
M.V.	20,000	
Current Assets		
Stock 1.1.	3,500	
Debtors	4,750	
Prepayments	200	
Bank	3,100	
Cash	100	
Purchases	20,050	
Expenses		
Administration	2,000	
Sales and Marketing	3,500	
Rent	3,200	
Bad Debts	150	
Returns In	150	
Creditors		4,250
Capital		100,000
Sales		35,000
Loan from Tootsie		19,180
Provisions:		
Bad Debts		50
Depreciation:		
L & B		25,000
Machinery		18,000
M.V.		8,000
Returns Out		130
Suspense A/c		990
	210,700	210,700

1) Stock at 31.12.84 £5,150.
2) Administration expenses incurred but not paid £250.
3) A credit sale £500 has been completely omitted from the books.

4) Sales & Marketing expenses overcast £550.
5) Administration expenses undercast £50.
6) Purchases have been overcast by £490.
7) Bad debt provision is to be made 2.5% of closing Debtor Balance.
8) Rent is payable at £250 per month throughout the year.
9) Depreciation is provided as follows:
   (1) L & B written off equally over 50 years.
   (2) Machinery written off 20% p.a. reducing balance.
   (3) M.V. written off 20% p.a. straight line.
10) Interest on loan is to be charged 10% p.a. on capital sum outstanding on loan at beginning of the year.
11) Capital repaid on loan in the year not included in the Trial Balance was £3,000.

You are required to:
1. Show the journals necessary to clear the Suspense Account.
2. Show the Suspense Account cleared.
3. Draw up a Trading and Profit and Loss Account for the year ended 31.12.1984.
4. Draw up a Balance Sheet as at 31.12.1984.

(20 marks)

QUESTION 24

EDGEWORTH

Edgeworth's profit is £7,600 on the Income Statement on the 30.6.84. The following information has since come to light.

1) Purchase of a motor van for £3,500 has been entered as Motor Vehicle expenses.
2) Motor vehicle repairs amounting to £750 have been entered in the fixed asset account.
3) Cost of a factory extension £5,000 has been entered in the fixed asset account for land and buildings.
4) Legal costs incurred on a factory extension amounting to £500 have been entered as a legal expense.

5) Depreciation is to be provided as follows:—
   Land & buildings   50 years   Straight Line Basis
   Motor vehicles   20% p.a.   Straight Line Basis

Required:
1) Journal entries to make any corrections you think are necessary.
2) A revised income statement to 30.6.84.   *(20 marks)*

QUESTION 25

The first draft of the final accounts of Torkard Traders disclosed a net profit of £41,004 and a capital employed of £352,600, before providing for the manager's efficiency bonus, but including £8,928 (credit balance) for errors held in suspense.

H. Huthwaithe, the manager, receives a basic salary plus an annual bonus of £300 for every complete percentage point by which the net profit to capital employed percentage exceeds 10%. In this context, net profit is before charging the manager's bonus, and capital employed is defined as fixed assets plus working capital. The bonus calculation is not carried out until the figures have been audited.

During the course of the audit, it was discovered that:

(i)   discounts allowed, £536, had been credited to discounts received;

(ii) the sale for cash, of some disused fixtures and fittings which had been completely written off in a previous year, had been credited to Fixtures and Fittings, £470;

(iii) an amount of £380 owed by M & Co. for goods supplied had been settled in contra against an amount of £850 owing to M & Co., but the ledger entries had not yet been made;

(iv) a glass carboy containing chemicals, which was kept in the warehouse, had sprung a leak. The resultant seepage had caused irreparable damage to stock valued at £800 but no account has yet been taken of this fact;

(v)   due to an oversight, credit sales for the last three days of the accounting year, amounting to £1,575, have been completely omitted from the Sales Day Book;

(vi)   in the Purchase Day Book, a sub-total of £27,183.54 had been carried forward as £37,183.54. Creditors, however, have been correctly posted;

(vii)   a credit sale invoice of £978 had been entered in the Sales Day Book as £789;

(viii)   a credit note from a supplier for £21 in respect of faulty goods, had not been posted;

(ix)   the proprietor of Torkard Traders sometimes, for his convenience, abstracts cash from the till for personal purposes. During the year, this has amounted to £86. The book-keeper states that he has 'reduced cash sales so that the cash book balances'.

Required:

(a)   Recalculate the net profit and capital employed figures after the above errors have been corrected.   *(16 marks)*

(b)   Calculate the manager's bonus.   *(4 marks)*

(c)   Open the Suspense account and post the eliminating entries.   *(3 marks)*

(Total 23 marks)

(ACCA)

QUESTION 26

INCOMPLETE RECORDS SECTION

After completing a training course at a technical college, Michael Faraday set up in business as a self-employed electrician on 1 January 1985.

He was very competent at his job but had no idea how to maintain proper accounting records. Sometime during 1985 one of his friends asked Michael how well his business was doing. He replied "All right . . . I think . . . but I'm not quite sure".

In the ensuing conversation his friend asked whether he had prepared accounts yet, covering his first quarter's trading, to which Michael replied that he had not. His friend then stressed that, for various reasons, it was vital for accounts of businesses to be prepared properly.

Shortly afterwards Michael came to see you to ask for your help in preparing accounts for his first quarter's trading. He brought with him, in a cardboard box, the only records he had, mainly scribbled on scraps of paper.

He explained that he started his business with a car worth £700, and £2,250 in cash of which £250 was his savings and £2,000 had been borrowed from a relative at an interest rate of 10% per annum. It was his practice to pay his suppliers and expenses in cash, to require his customers to settle their accounts in cash and to bank any surplus in a business bank account. He maintained lists of cash receipts and cash payments, of supplies obtained on credit and of work carried out for customers and of appliances sold, on credit.

The list of credit suppliers comprised:

Date supplied	Supplier	Amount owed	Date paid	Amount paid	Remarks
1985		£	1985	£	
January	Dee & Co.	337.74	March	330.00	Received discount £7.74
	AB Supplies	528.20	March	528.20	
February	Simpson	141.34	March	138.00	Received discount £3.34
	Cotton Ltd	427.40	March	130.00	Payment on account
			April	297.40	Remainder
	Dee & Co.	146.82	March	140.00	Received discount £6.82
March	AB Supplies	643.43	April	643.43	
	Simpson	95.60			Not yet paid

The purchase in January from Dee & Co. was of tools and equipment to enable him to carry out electrical repair work. All the remaining purchases were of repair materials, except for the purchase in February from Cotton Ltd. which consisted entirely of electrical appliances for resale.

In addition to the above credit transactions, he had bought repair materials for cash, as follows:

1985	£
January	195.29
February	161.03
March	22.06

Other cash payments comprised:

1985		£
January	Rent of premises for January to June 1985	400.00
	Rates of premises for January to March 1985	150.00
	Stationery	32.70
	Car running expenses	92.26
February	Sundries	51.54
	Car running expenses	81.42
March	Sundries	24.61
	Car running expenses	104.52
	Transfer to bank	500.00

He had also withdrawn £160.00 in cash at the end of each month for living expenses.

The list of credit customers comprised:

Date of sale 1985	Customer	Amount owed £	Date received 1985	Amount received £	Remarks
January	D. Hopkins	362.80	February	357.00	Allowed discount £5.80
	P. Bolton	417.10	March	417.10	
February	G. Leivers	55.00	March	55.00	
	M. Whitehead	151.72	April	151.72	
	N. John Ltd.	49.14	April	49.14	
	A. Linneker	12.53	March	12.53	
March	E. Horton	462.21	April	462.21	
	S. Ward	431.08	March	426.00	Allowed discount £5.08
	W. Scothern & Co	319.12			Not yet received
	N. Annable	85.41			Not yet received

The above amounts relate to charges for repair work which he had carried out, except that the amounts shown in February for G. Leivers, N. John Ltd. and A. Linneker are for sales of electrical appliances.

In addition to the above credit transactions, he had cash takings, as follows:

1985		£
January	Repair work	69.44
February	Repair work	256.86
March	Repair work	182.90
	Appliances	112.81

He estimated that, at the end of March 1985, his stock of electrical repair materials was £691.02 and of electrical appliances for resale was £320.58, his tools and equipment were worth £300.00 and his car, £600.00

Apart from loan interest, the only accrual was for heating and lighting, £265.00.

Required:

(a) Prepare
    (i) purchase daybook with analysis columns for type of purchase, and
    (ii) sales daybook with analysis columns for class of business undertaken. *(6 marks)*

(b) Open, post to 31 March 1985 only, and balance a columnar cash book suitably analysed to facilitate ledger postings. *(8 marks)*

(c) Open, post to 31 March 1985 only, and balance a creditors ledger control account and a debtors ledger control account. Use the closing balances in your answer to (g) below. (N.B. Individual accounts for creditors and debtors are **NOT** required). *(3 marks)*

(d) Open, post and balance sales and cost of sales accounts, each with separate columns for "Repairs" and "Appliances". *(3 marks)*

(e) Prepare M. Faraday's trading account for the quarter ended 31 March 1985, distinguishing between gross profit on repairs and on appliance sales. *(3 marks)*

(f) Prepare M. Faraday's general profit and loss account for the quarter ended 31 March 1985. *(4 marks)*

(g) Prepare M. Faraday's balance sheet as at 31 March 1985. *(7 marks)*

(Total 34 marks)

(ACCA)

QUESTION 27

INCOMPLETE RECORDS — USING RATIOS

For a number of years Martin Smith has been employed as the works' manager of a company which manufactures cardboard cartons.

He has now decided to leave the company and to set up a similar business of his own on 1 January 1986 but, before taking this step he wants to see what his financial results are likely to be for his first year of operations.

In order to do this, he has obtained certain "average industry" ratios from his trade association, the Cardboard Carton Manufacturers' Association (CCMA), which he wants to use as his norm for predicting the first year's results.

At this stage he consults you, asks for your professional assistance and supplies the following information.

	CCMA statistics 1984 (based on year-end figures)
Sales/Net assets employed	2.8 times
Gross profit/Sales	28.0%
Net profit/Sales	10.0%
Fixed assets/Working capital	1.5:1
Current assets/Current liabilities	2.25:1
Debtors collection period	36.5 days
Creditors payment period	58.4 days

He informs you that he is able to contribute £40,000 as capital and has been promised a long term loan of £6,000 from a relative.

Initially, he intends to acquire a stock of materials at a cost of £20,000 but his (simple) average stock for the first year will be £18,500. Purchases of materials for the year, excluding the initial purchase of stock, £20,000, will be £97,800. All purchases and sales will be on credit.

Sundry accruals at 31 December 1986 are estimated at £350 and bank and cash balances at £5,000.

He proposes to withdraw £10,000 during the year for living expenses.

Required:

Prepare, in as much detail as can be elicited from the information supplied, a forecast trading and profit and loss account for Martin Smith's proposed business for the year ended 31 December 1986, and a forecast balance sheet at that date. All figures should be stated to the nearest £10. Marks will be awarded for workings which must be shown. *(18 marks)*

(ACCA)

QUESTION 28

Gillespie was a sole trader in a retail business, all sales being made for cash. His draft balance sheet on Friday, 30 June 1984 was as follows:

	£		£	£
Fixtures and fittings	2,800	Capital account		9,000
Stock, at		Current account		1,000
cost	7,200	Creditors:		
Balance at		Trade	1,360	
bank	1,960	Expenses	680	
Cash in hand	80			2,040
	12,040			12,040

Exactly eight weeks later, on the night of Friday 25 August 1984, a fire occurred which destroyed all his stock, fixtures and fittings, financial books, records and papers, with the exception of the file of unpaid invoices and the cash box containing the unbanked cash that he had taken home with him.

His fire insurance policy included cover of his stock, at cost, not exceeding £10,000 and fixtures and fittings at an agreed value £2,700. He had not insured against loss of profit.

The cash in hand on 30 June 1984 and all takings up to the close of business on 25 August 1984 had been banked with the exception of:
(a) £24 per week paid as wages;
(b) £30 per week that he had withdrawn for personal expenses; and
(c) £120 in the cash box taken home with him.

All payments for goods and business expenses, other than wages, were made by cheque.

The selling price of his goods was obtained by adding 30% to the cost price.

An analysis of his bank statement for the eight weeks ended 25 August 1984 showed the following receipts and payments:

	£
Receipts:	
Cash banked	5,768
Payments:	
Creditors for goods supplied	2,800
Expenses	920

The total of unpaid invoices on 25 August 1984 amounted to:

Goods	1,120
Expenses	280

You are required to prepare:

(a) a statement setting out his claim for loss of stock; and *(15 marks)*

(b) a profit and loss account for the eight weeks ended 25 August 1984, and a balance sheet on that date assuming the claims for loss of stock and fixtures and fittings are admitted. *(15 marks)*

QUESTION 29

Ricky is in business on his own account. On December 31st he invites good customers and friends to his premises to celebrate his first year in business. The party finished at 8.00 p.m. Ricky and some of the guests went on to a club. On arriving home at 3.00 a.m., he noticed a police car outside his house. The policeman greeted him with the news that his premises had been burnt to the ground. The suspected cause being a lighted cigarette left in some accounting ledgers. He was most distressed and immediately rang his accountant to tell him of the problem. The accountant, being a sympathetic chap, told him not to worry since he felt sure he would be able to reconstruct some financial statements from the business bank account and information that Ricky himself would be able to supply. At the meeting on the next day, the following information came to light:—

1.

	£ 31.12.84	£ 31.12.85
Stock	5,250	4,375
Debtors	4,950	5,260
Bank	3,200	?
Cash	500	?
Fixed Assets		
Premises Net Book Value (NBV)	15,000	?
Motor Van Net Book Value (NBV)	5,000	?
Creditors	4,850	5,315

2. All business transactions apart from one or two specific items which Ricky had a note of, passed through the business bank account. Together the accountant and Ricky quickly obtained totals for the following:—
   a) Payments to creditors during the year amounted to £37,550.
   b) Payments received from debtors £72,340.
   c) Weekly wages paid £60 per week for 52 weeks.
   d) Rates £1,200.
   e) Electricity for light and heat in the respect of the period 30 September 1985 — £900. The bill for the final quarter had not yet been received.
   f) Advertising expenditure — £2,250 for the year.
   g) Postage and stationery totalled £750 for the year, however, on investigating the premises during the morning after the fire, the franking machine was found intact and the meter showed that £49 of postage stamps was still unused.
   h) Ricky subscribed to a trade association. The fee is £20 each year. He has not paid his subscription for the year to December '85 as yet but he intends to. Furthermore, he did not pay his '84 subscription until Feb. '85.
   i) Ricky received cash from sales £150 on 31.12.85 which he took home with him.
   l) Road Tax for the year, paid by cheque in January, was £85 and Insurance £120.
   j) Payments made by cheque to the local garage for petrol totalled £720 for the year. The last payment on this petrol

account was made during October in respect of the quarter to the 30 September '85. The final quarter's bill has not yet been made.

* No depreciation has been charged for the year in respect of premises or the motor van. The premises are to be depreciated by 2% on the net book value for the previous year. The motor van is to be depreciated by 20% per annum on the previous year's NBV.

The Insurance company is expected to settle the claim on the basis of the accounts submitted by Ricky.

Required:

You are required to:—

1. Prepare a Trading, Profit & Loss Account for the year ended 31.12.85.
2. Construct a Balance Sheet as at that date.
   Note, however, before you can do so you will need to take the following appropriate steps:—
   1. Prepare a Bank and Cash Control Account for the year '85.
   2. Prepare an Opening Statement of Affairs (Capital).
   3. Prepare Debtors and Creditors Control Account (Sales & Purchases figures).
   4. Make appropriate adjustments.

QUESTION 30

Victor Bingham commenced business as a retail grocer on 1st November 1980 but has not kept a proper set of books of account. Most of his sales are for cash and a record of credit sales has been maintained.

A summary of the bank transactions for the year to 31st October 1981 is as follows:—

Lodgements	£Dr	Payments	£Cr
Introduction of Capital	18,600	Fixtures & Fittings	8,005
Receipts from Credit Sales	18,178	Vehicles	4,000
Net Cash Sales (i.e. after		Stationery & Advertising	1,488
payments)	86,800	Personal Expenses	930
		Electricity	521
		Purchases for Resale	92,008
		Staff Wages	8,184
		Rent & Rates	2,108
		Insurance	620
		Legal Costs	645

In addition to making the following cash payments before banking the takings, Bingham also withdrew £110 each for living expenses.

Cash Payments	£
Sundry Expenses	496
Purchases for Resale	248
Staff Wages & Insurance	2,654

The following additional information is also available:—

(a)

	31.10.81
	£
Stock on hand	9,920
Debtors	2,554
Creditors	5,456
Heating & Lighting Accrued (Electricity)	136
Rates Paid in Advance	164
Insurance Paid in Advance	10

(b) Goods costing £960 had been taken by Bingham from stock for his own use, and depreciation is to be provided for at the rate of 20% on cost price per annum on fixtures and fittings, and on motor vehicles.

(c) Assume a 52 week year.

Required:

You are required to:

1. Prepare cash and bank accounts covering the year ended 31st October 1981. *(10 marks)*
2. Prepare a Trading and Profit and Loss Account for the year ended 31st October 1981, together with a Balance Sheet as at that date. *(20 marks)*

(Total 30 marks)

(AAT)

QUESTION 31

David Denton set up in business as a plumber a year ago, and he has asked you to act as his accountant. His instructions to you are in the form of the following letter:—

Dear Henry,

I was pleased when you agreed to act as my accountant and look forward to your first visit to check my records. The proposed fee of £250 p.a. is acceptable. I regret that the paperwork for the work done during the year is incomplete. I started my business on 1 January last, and put £6,500 into a business bank account on that date. I brought my van into the firm at that time, and reckon that it was worth £3,600 then. I think it will last another three years after the end of the first year of business use.

I have drawn £90 per week from the business bank account during the year. In my trade it is difficult to take a holiday, but my wife managed to get away for a while. The travel agent's bill for £280 was paid out of the business account. I bought the lease of the yard and office for £6,500. The lease has ten years to run, and the rent is only £300 a year payable in advance on the anniversary of the date of purchase, which was 1 April. I borrowed £4,000 on that day from Aunt Jane to help pay for the lease. I have agreed to pay her 10% interest per annum, but have been too busy to do anything about this yet.

I was lucky enough to meet Miss Prism shortly before I set up on my own, and she has worked for me as an office organiser right from the start. She is paid a salary of £3,000 p.a. All the bills for the year have been carefully preserved in a tool box, and we analysed them last week. The materials I have bought cost me £9,600, but I reckon there was £580 worth left in the yard on 31 December. I have not paid for them all yet, I think we owed £714 to the suppliers on 31 December. I was surprised to see that I had spent £4,800 on plumbing equipment, but it should last me five years or so. Electricity bills received up to 30 September came to £1,122; but motor expenses were £912, and general expenses £1,349 for the year. The insurance premium for the year to 31 March next was £800. All these have been paid by cheque but Miss Prism has lost the rate demand. I expect the Local Authority will send a reminder soon since I have not yet paid. I seem to remember that rates came to £180 for the year to 31 March next.

Miss Prism sent out bills to my customers for work done, but some of them are very slow to pay. Altogether the charges made were £29,863, but only £25,613 had been received by 31 December. Miss Prism thinks that 10% of the remaining bills are not likely to be paid. Other customers for jobs too small to bill have paid £3,418 in cash for work done, but I only managed to bank £2,600 of this money. I used £400 of the difference to pay the family's grocery bills, and Miss Prism used the rest for general expenses, except for £123 which was left over in a drawer in the office on 31 December.

Kind regards,
Yours sincerely,
David.

Required:

You are required to draw up a Profit and Loss Account for the year ended 31 December, and a Balance Sheet as at that date.

(22 marks)

(ACCA)

QUESTION 32

JERRY MANDA — Stock Valuation

Jerry Manda trades in paint as a retailer. You may assume that all his issues are sold. The following transactions take place during 1985:

1st Jan.	20 units a £20 each	(STOCK AT START)
1st Jun.	15 units a £25 each	
30th Sept.	10 units a £30 each	PURCHASES
31st Dec.	20 units a £32 each	

1st Jun.	16 units	
30th Sept.	12 units	ISSUES
31st Dec.	22 units	

The selling price per unit is £32.

Required:
1) Using the perpetual inventory method, calculate the Gross Profit using LIFO, FIFO and AVCO.
2) Briefly explain your findings.

(16 marks)

QUESTION 33

The draft accounts of the Flaker Airfreight Company for the year to 30 June 1984 are as follows:

	1984		1983	
	£	£	£	£
Balance sheet				
Freehold premises at cost		250,000		150,000
Plant, at cost	420,000		250,000	
Less Depreciation	160,000		110,000	
		260,000		140,000
Debtors		160,000		120,000
Stock		240,000		200,000
		910,000		610,000
Capital		690,000		440,000
Long-term loans		100,000		100,000
Trade creditors		90,000		60,000
Bank overdraft		30,000		10,000
		910,000		610,000
Profit and loss account				
Sales revenue		1,050,000		850,000
Trading profit		157,000		122,000
Less Depreciation	50,000		40,000	
Loan interest	7,000		7,000	
	-	57,000		47,000
Net profit for the year		100,000		75,000

Required:

(a) Rearrange the above Balance Sheets of Flaker Airfreight into a presentable format. *(4 marks)*

(b) Draw up a Statement of Sources and Application of Funds for the year ended 30 June 1984. *(16 marks)*

(c) Show your workings clearly where appropriate on a separate working paper. *(4 marks)*

(d) Briefly comment upon the change in working capital over the year. You may use working capital ratios to support your analysis. *(6 marks)*

(Total 30 marks)

QUESTION 34

1. From the following information prepare a Cash Budget for 3 months to 30th June 1984 and a forecast Profit and Loss Statement for the 3 months to 30th June 1984.
2. State briefly why the cash balance at the end is different from the profit figure. *(30 marks)*

(1) The cash balance at the start on 1.4.84 is £1,500.

(2) Sales are made on credit terms, payment being received in the month after the point of sale.

	Mar. £	Apr. £	May £	June £	July £
Sales	5000	3500	4500	5500	6000

(3) Creditors for stock in trade are paid one month after the purchases have been received.

	Mar. £	Apr. £	May £	June £	July £
Creditors at month end	2000	2500	1500	3000	2500

N.B. (i) The opening stock on 1.4.84 is £2,000.
(ii) The Gross Margin on Sales is 50%.

(4) Wages **are paid one month in arrears** i.e. wages are paid on the last day of the month following that in which they were earned, and the charge for each month was as follows:

	Mar. £	Apr. £	May £	June £	July £
Wages	800	700	900	800	800

(5) All expenses are paid in the month in which they are incurred:

	Mar. £	Apr. £	May £	June £	July £
Advertising	500	750	500	500	750
Repairs	100	90	100	80	100
Secretarial	150	150	150	150	150

(6) Depreciation is charged on fixed assets at 20% per annum on cost. The cumulative depreciation charged stands at £4,000 on 1.4.84 and the Net Book Value of assets at that date is £6,000.

QUESTION 35

A. Kennedy commences in business on the 1st January; he has £6,000 of cash to start with. On 1st January he buys a machine for £3,600 which he expects to last 4 years. He pays for the machine in three equal instalments commencing on 1st January, 1st February, 1st March. He buys stock for resale on 1st January, £3,000. Payments need to be made one month in arrears. He pays the following expenses cash each month:

Wages	£200
Rent	£100
Other	£200

He makes the following sales on credit terms:

January	£3,000
February	£2,000
March	£5,000

Debtors pay one month after the month of sale. The margin is 50%. He buys more stock in February on the same credit terms as before, £2,000 and in March £3,000.

Required:

1) A cash budget for the 3 months to March 31st.
2) A budgeted profit statement for the 3 months to 31/3.
3) A brief explanation as to why the closing cash figure differs from the profit figure.

(20 marks)

QUESTION 36

Mountfield Ltd. Balance Sheet at 31.12.84

	£Cost	£Depn.	£NBV
Fixed Assets			
Land & Buildings	50,000	5,000	45,000
Motor Vehicles	15,000	3,000	12,000
	65,000	8,000	57,000
Current Assets			
Stock	5,500		
Debtors	3,100		
Bank & Cash	1,500		
		10,100	
Less Current Liabilities			
Creditors	2,900		
Taxation	1,000		
Proposed Dividend	1,000		
		4,900	
Net Current Assets			5,200
TOTAL NET ASSETS			62,200
Financed by			
Share Capital £1 Ordinary Shares		50,000	
P/L Reserve		12,200	
Capital Employed			62,200

NOTES

1) It is estimated that the following transactions will take place during the first 3 months of 1985:

Sales	Jan.	4,000
	Feb.	5,000
	Mar.	7,000

2) Debtors will pay 1 month in arrears.
3) Stock Purchases will be:

	Jan.	4,000
	Feb.	2,000
	Mar.	2,000

Trade creditors will be paid 1 month after the month of purchase.
4) The mark-up on goods sold is 60% of the cost price.
5) Last year's tax of £1,000 will be paid in the month of March in cash.
6) Last year's proposed dividend will also be paid in March in cash.
7) It is estimated that a new share issue will be made in January of 10,000 £1 Ordinary shares at par.
8) New plant and machinery will be purchased on the 1st of January for £10,000.
9) Expenses will be paid in the month in which they fall.
10) Wages £1,000 paid in cash.
11) General expenses £500.
12) Depreciation is as follows:
Land & Building written off equally over 50 years.
Motor Vehicle 20% p.a. on a straight line basis.
Plant and Machinery 10% p.a. on a straight line basis.
13) Land and Building costing £10,000 will be sold for an estimated £15,000 cash on 31st March. They were bought on the 1st April, 1980.
14) A provision for doubtful debts is to be made equivalent to 2% of the closing debtor balance.

Required

1) A cash flow forecast for the 3 months to 31 March 1985.
2) A budgeted Profit and Loss statement for same period.
3) A budget Balance Sheet as at 31.3.85.
4) A forecast source and application of funds statement for the year.

5) You are required to analyse the two financial statements using the following ratios to help you.
   1. The rate of stock turnover.
   2. Debtors to sales.
   3. Creditors to purchases.
   4. Gross Profit to Sales ratio.
   5. Net Profit to Sales ratio.
   6. The quick ratio Current Assets to Current Liabilities.
   7. The Acid test ratio current asset — stocks to current liabilities.
   8. Return on Capital Employed, i.e. Net Profit to Capital Employed.

(30 marks)

QUESTION 37

ZERO LTD. — Summarised Trading & P/L Account

	31.5.83 £		31.5.84 £
Sales		30,000		34,000
Cost of Sales			
Opening Stock	8,000		10,000
Purchases	22,000		30,000
Closing Stock	10,000		15,000
		20,000		25,000
Gross Profit		10,000		9,000
Less Expenses		8,000		9,100
Net Profit		2,000		(100)

ZERO LTD. — Balance Sheet Summaries

	31.5.83 £		31.5.84 £
FIXED ASSETS			
Cost	100,000		100,000
Depreciation	40,000		62,000
NBV		60,000		48,000
CURRENT ASSETS			
Stock	10,000		15,000
Debtors	5,000		9,000
Cash	500		400
	15,500		24,400
CURRENT LIABILITIES			
Trade Creditors	6,000		4,000
Other Creditors	1,000		—
Net Current Assets		8,500		20,400
		68,500		68,400
FINANCED BY			
£1 Ordinary Shares		50,000		50,000
PROFIT and LOSS RESERVE		18,500		18,400
		68,500		68,400

You are required to:—

1. From the above summarised Balance Sheets and Trading and Profit & Loss Accounts for two years of Zero Ltd., you are required to advise the management about their performance. Use and explain the purpose of any accounting ratios you consider useful in your analysis.
2. The management of working capital is often said by businessmen to be the most important factor to control in order to control the business. Explain what working capital is and say what you understand by this statement.
3. Explain the term RESERVE as used in accounting.

(30 marks)

QUESTION 38

The net assets of three unconnected companies are financed as follows, as at 31 December 1984:

	X PLC		Company Y PLC		Z PLC	
	£000	£000	£000	£000	£000	£000
Share capital						
Authorised						
Ordinary shares of £1.00 per share		12,000		—		—
Ordinary shares of £0.25 per share		—		6,000		6,000
8% preference shares of £1.00 per share		—		4,000		4,000
		12,000		10,000		10,000
Called up and issued						
Ordinary shares of £1.00 per share £0.75 paid		6,000	—		—	
Ordinary shares of £0.25 per share fully paid		—	4,000		1,000	
8% preference shares of £1.00 per share, fully paid		—	4,000		2,000	
		6,000		8,000		3,000
Reserves						
Share premium account (raised on issue of ordinary shares)			500		200	
General reserve	1,000		—		1,300	
Fixed asset revaluation reserve	2,000		—		—	
Fixed asset replacement reserve	—		1,000		—	
Profit and loss account	1,000		500		1,500	
		4,000		2,000		3,000
Shareholders' funds		10,000		10,000		6,000
10% Debenture stock		—		—		4,000
		10,000		10,000		10,000

For all three companies, the profit before interest and tax is estimated at £5,000,000 for the next 12 months ended 31 December 1985. The capital structure of each company will remain unaltered.

Taxation on profits after interest is an effective rate of 40%. Assume that an ordinary dividend of 12% of the paid up share capital will be paid.

Required:
For each of the three companies,
(a) prepare the estimated profit and loss accounts for the year ended 31 December 1985,   *(4 marks)*
(b) calculate
    (i) basic earnings per share for the year ended 31 December 1985,
    (ii) gearing ratio as at 31 December 1984,   *(8 marks)*
(c) briefly explain, in relation to gearing, the effects on earnings of substantial changes in profit after tax.
                                                        (4 marks)

Marks will be awarded for workings which must be shown.   *(Total 16 marks)*

(ACCA)

QUESTION 39

Rock commenced business on 1 September 1983 selling televisions and videos on cash and hire purchase terms. The following summarized trial balance was extracted from his books of account as at 31 August 1984:

	£ Dr	£ Cr
Bank overdraft		8,475
Capital (cash introduced on 1 September 1983)		50,000
Cash sales: televisions (600 at £300 each)		180,000
Creditors		121,000
Debtors	1,000	
Drawings	16,000	
Fixed assets at cost	45,000	
Hire purchase debtors: televisions	105,000	
videos	342,000	
Hire purchase sales: televisions (350 at £400 each)		140,000
Hire purchase sales: videos (380 at £1,260 each)		478,800
Purchases:		
televisions (1,000 at £150 each)	150,000	
videos (400 at £350 each)	140,000	
Retailing expenses	179,275	
	£978,275	£978.275

Additional information

1. During the year, Rock purchased 1,000 televisions at a cost of £150 each. He sold them either on cash terms for £300 each or on hire purchase. The hire purchase terms were an initial deposit of £100, followed by two annual instalments of £150 each, payable by the customer on the first and second anniversary respectively of the date of purchase of the television.

2. Rock had also purchased 400 videos for £350 each. Although he was prepared to sell them on cash terms (for £1,000 each), all the video sales had been on hire purchase. An initial deposit of £360 was required, followed by two annual instalments of £450 each, payable by the customer on the first and second anniversary respectively of the date of purchase of the video.

3. In the annual accounts, Rock decided to take credit for gross profit on hire purchase sales in accordance with the following policy:

a) televisions: to allow for both the ordinary gross profit and hire purchase interest in proportion to the total cash collected from customers sold televisions on hire purchase terms; and

b) videos: to take the ordinary gross profit on videos sold on hire purchase in the year of sale, and to apportion the interest on hire purchase equally over the two years of the agreement.

4. Depreciation is to be provided on fixed assets at 20% per annum on cost.

Required:

a) Prepare columnar trading, profit and loss accounts for the year to 31 August 1984, and a balance sheet as at that date, for
   i)   televisions,
   ii) videos, and
   iii) the business as a whole, and a combined profit and loss account for the year to 31 August 1984.   *(17 marks)*

b) Prepare a balance sheet as at 31 August 1984. *(8 marks)*

(Total 25 marks)

(AAT)

QUESTION 40

Lennon Limited was set up on 1st January 1985 with a share capital of £100,000 and loan capital £25,000. It purchased fixed assets, having an estimated useful life of eight years, for £80,000 and commenced trading. The financial statements prepared on an Historic Cost basis for the first year are given below:—

LENNON LIMITED

Historic Profit and Loss Account
for the year ended 31.12.83.

	£	£
Sales		180,000
Less cost of sales		80,000
Gross profit		100,000
Less Operating expense	40,000	
Depreciation	10,000	
		50,000
Net operating profit (before interest and dividends)		50,000
Less interest		2,500
Net profit attributable to shareholders		47,500
Dividend paid		12,500
Retained profit		£35,000

LENNON LIMITED

Historic Cost Balance Sheet
as at 31.12.83.

	£ Cost	£ Depreciation	£ N.B.V.
Fixed Assets	80,000	10,000	70,000
Current Assets			
Stock	50,000		
Debtors	30,000		
Cash	30,000		
		110,000	
Less Current Liabilities			
Creditors		20,000	
			90,000
			£160,000
Financed By:			
Share Capital			100,000
Reserves (P/L)			35,000
Shareholders' Funds			135,000
Debentures			25,000
			£160,000

The following additional information is also available:—

1. Stock prices rose evenly by 15% during the year. Average Stock Turnover is three times per annum.
2. Replacement Fixed Assets of the type purchased on 1st January would have cost £96,000 on 31st December.

3. Stock prices had risen by 2% over the period represented by the average age of debtors and creditors.

Required:
You are required to prepare financial statements for Lennon Limited in accordance with the standard Statement of Accounting Practice on Current Cost Accounting (SSAP 16).

(30 marks)

QUESTION 41
The cash book, bank columns, for January 1984, of S. Simpson, sole trader is as follows:—

1984		£	1984		£
1 January	Balance	1,507.71	2 January	Electricity Board	43.10
9 January	Sales	1,370.00	2 January	John Jones Ltd.	149.10
17 January	Sales	168.54	4 January	Printers' Supplies Ltd	29.30
23 January	T. White Ltd.	310.00	5 January	Kingsway Products	37.08
24 January	Sales	150.00	12 January	Harold Smith Ltd.	138.32
30 January	Sales	44.70	17 January	Gray's Machines Ltd.	645.10
31 January	Sales	210.00	24 January	Giant Displays	70.56
			26 January	P. Swann	124.64
			30 January	Deposit account	2,000.00
			30 January	Wages	320.40
			31 January	Balance	203.35
		£3,760.95			£3,760.95

On 6 February 1984, S. Simpson received his bank statement
for the previous month; the bank statement was as follows:
*Mr. S. Simpson – Statement of account with North Bank PLC.,
Main Street Branch, Westford.*

Date 1984	Particulars	Payments £	Receipts £	Balance £
1 January	Balance			1,468.21
3 January	Bank Giro Credit		100.00	1,568.21
4 January	145688	149.10		1,419.11
5 January	145686	60.50		1,358.61
6 January	Charges	15.40		1,343.21
9 January	Standing order	12.00		1,331.21
10 January	Bank Giro Credit		1,370.00	2,701.21
11 January	145687	43.10		2,658.11
13 January	145690	37.08		2,621.03
17 January	Sundry Credit		168.54	2,789.57
18 January	145691	138.32		2,651.25
20 January	145689	29.30		2,651.95
23 January	Sundry Credit		310.00	2,931.95
26 January	Standing Order	44.00		2,887.95
27 January	Bank Giro Credit		150.00	3,037.95
30 January	Deposit account	2,000.00		1,037.95
30 January	Sundry Credit		44.70	1,082.65
31 January	145693	70.56		1,012.09

On 8 February 1984, S. Simpson discovers that the sales
debited in the cash book on 31 January 1984 should read
"£230.00" not "£210.00" and is advised by the bank that the
standing order charge of £44.00 on 26 January was made in
error and that the bank account has now been credited with
£44.00.

Required:
Prepare a bank reconciliation statement as at 31 January 1984.

(20 marks)

(AAT)

QUESTION 42

You are presented with the Bank Statement of McCartney, a sole trader, and a summary of his Bank Receipts and Payments for the month of January.

McCARTNEY — Summarized Bank Transactions for January
BANK ACCOUNT — Nominal Ledger

Date	Account Name	£Dr	Date	Account Name	£Cr
1.1	Balance b/f	2,500	1.1	A Ltd. — Creditor	500
	A. Jones — Debtor	1,000		Cheque No. (001)	
	S. Murphy — Debtor	1,250		Wages — Cheque (002)	600
	P. Parfitt — Debtor	750		Advertising — Cheque (003)	300
				JKS Ltd. — Creditor	
				Cheque (004)	500
			31.1	Balance c/f	3,600
		5,500			5,500

McCARTNEY — Bank Statement

Date	Detail	£Dr	£Cr	£Balance
1.1	Balance b/f		2,500	2,500 Cr
	Sundry Credit — A. Jones		1,000	3,500 Cr
	Cheque 001	500		3,000 Cr
	Cheque 003	300		2,700 Cr
	Cheque 004	500		2,200 Cr
	Sundry Credit — S. Murphy		1,250	3,450 Cr
	Bank Charges	25		3,425 Cr
	Standing Order — Rent	25		3400 Cr
	Direct Debits	50		3,350 Cr
	Bank Giro Credit — Smith		100	3,450 Cr

Required:

You are required to:—

1. Draw up a Bank Reconciliation Statement for the month of January. *(14 marks)*
2. Give six reasons why differences may occur between the business organization records (i.e. Bank Account — Cash Book) and the Bank's Statement. *(6 marks)*

(Total 20 marks)

QUESTION 43

ADF Ltd. dispose of motor vehicles shown at cost in the balance sheet at 30.6. at £7,000. The cumulative depreciation provided against those vehicles to 30.6. was £4,000. The proceeds of the disposal was received by cheque £5,100 on that day.

Required:

You are required to:—

(a) Show the Journal Entries required to record the above events.

(b) Show the Profit or Loss on Disposal in a Disposal Account.

(16 marks)

MULTIPLE CHOICE
QUESTION 44

Name the four fundamental concepts which are the subject of Standard Statement of Accounting Practice (SSAP 2) No.2.

QUESTION 45

Fixed Assets are best described as:
(a) Land and Buildings
(b) Those assets which a business intends to keep and use to produce revenue over a number of years.
(c) Assets which do not move.
(d) Plant and Machinery.
(e) Those assets which are regarded as capital investment.

QUESTION 46

Current Assets are best described as:
(a) Assets currently in use.
(b) Stock and Debtors.
(c) Those assets which a business intends to use within a period of twelve months, e.g. Stock, Debtors, Bank and Cash.
(d) Working Capital.
(e) Net Current Assets.

QUESTION 47

Current Liabilities are best described as:
(a) Those liabilities which are payable immediately.
(b) Those liabilities which will be paid within 5 years.
(c) Those liabilities which will be paid within a period of twelve months.
(d) Creditors.
(e) Long term Loans.

QUESTION 48

The Margin is best described as:—

(a) $\dfrac{\text{Gross Profit}}{\text{Sales}} \times \dfrac{100}{1}$

(b) $\dfrac{\text{Cost of Sales}}{\text{Sales}} \times \dfrac{100}{1}$

(c) $\dfrac{\text{Sales}}{\text{Gross Profit}} \times \dfrac{100}{1}$

(d) $\dfrac{\text{Net Profit}}{\text{Gross Profit}} \times \dfrac{100}{1}$

(e) $\dfrac{\text{Sales}}{\text{Cost of Sales}} \times \dfrac{100}{1}$

QUESTION 49

The Mark Up is best described as:—

(a) $\dfrac{\text{Profit}}{\text{Selling Price}} \times \dfrac{100}{1}$

(b) $\dfrac{\text{Gross Profit}}{\text{Cost of Sales}} \times \dfrac{100}{1}$

(c) $\dfrac{\text{Net Profit}}{\text{Gross Profit}} \times \dfrac{100}{1}$

(d) $\dfrac{\text{Gross Profit}}{\text{Sales}} \times \dfrac{100}{1}$

(e) $\dfrac{\text{Sales}}{\text{Cost of Sales}} \times \dfrac{100}{1}$

QUESTION 50

CAPITAL is best described as:—
(a) The funds that the owners' of a business have invested in it.
(b) Fixed Assets
(c) Cash
(d) Stock and Cash
(e) Profit

QUESTION 51

LONG TERM LIABILITIES are best described as:—
(a) Those liabilities which are not current and which will be paid over periods longer than one year.
(b) Those liabilities which are not current.
(c) Debentures.
(d) Long Term Loans.
(e) Bank Overdrafts.

QUESTION 52

CAPITAL EMPLOYED is best described as:—
(a) Fixed Assets and Current Assets.
(b) All the money used in a business.
(c) Owners' funds plus profits retained plus any Loans the business has.
(d) Everything the business has.
(e) Money invested in the bank.

QUESTION 53

GROSS PROFIT is best described as:—
(a) The trading profit or loss.
(b) Sales Revenue less the Cost of Goods sold in a period.
(c) Sales Revenue less all costs.
(d) The profit after all expenses are paid.
(e) The Cost of Sales Account.

QUESTION 54

The Balance to carry forward on a Sales Ledger Control Account is:—
(a) The Total Purchases.
(b) The Total Sales
(c) The Total for Debits and Credits.
(d) The Total Creditors.
(e) The Total Debtors outstanding.

QUESTION 55

Given opening debtors b/f £8,500, sales £20,000 and the balance to c/f £5,000 the amounts received from debtors in the period must have been:—
(a) £25,000
(b) £20,000
(c) £15,000
(d) £28,500
(e) £23,500

QUESTION 56

The Sales Day Book may also be called:—
(a) The Purchase Day Book.
(b) The Sales Ledger.
(c) The Debtors Control Account.
(d) The Sales Journal.
(e) The Sales Invoice.

QUESTION 57

Sales Invoices are first entered into:—
(a) The Purchase Day Book.
(b) The Journal.
(c) The Cash Book.
(d) The Debtors Control Account.
(e) The Sales Day Book.

QUESTION 58

A debit balance in the cash book of £500 brought forward at the start of a period shows that:—
(a) Cash had been overspent by £500.
(b) The total cash spent was £500.
(c) The total cash received was £500.
(d) The business has £500 cash in hand.
(e) None of these.

QUESTION 59

A credit balance in the cash book of £100 brought forward at the start of a period shows that:—
(a) Cash had been overspent by £100.
(b) The total cash paid out was £100.
(c) The total cash received was £100.
(d) The business has £100 cash in hand.
(e) None of these.

QUESTION 60

An invoiced amount owing at the end of an accounting period is described as:—
(a) A Prepayment.
(b) An Asset.
(c) Debtors.
(d) An Accrual.
(e) None of these.

QUESTION 61

An invoice paid in respect of a future accounting period may be described as:—
(a) An Accrual.
(b) Creditors.
(c) A Liability.
(d) A Prepayment.
(e) None of these.

QUESTION 62

Cagney Ltd make one product which sells currently at £12 per unit. Direct Labour costs £5 per unit and Direct Materials cost £4 per unit. The Fixed Overheads for the year are estimated to be £1,500.

From the above information you are required to:—
(1) Calculate the contribution to fixed overheads.

(2½ marks)
(2) Calculate the required output to break-even. *(2½ marks)*
(3) Prepare a budgeted profit statement for the year at an output level of 550 units.   *(5 marks)*
(4) Give the 'margin of safety' at 550 units of output.

(2½ marks)
(5) Draw a Break-Even Chart which clearly shows:—
    (a) The Break-Even Point.
    (b) The Margin of Safety at 550 units of output.

(10 marks)
(6) Draw a Profit/Volume Graph which clearly shows:—
    (a) The Break-Even Point.
    (b) The Margin of Safety at 550 units of output.

(10 marks)
(7) Calculate the Profit/Volume Ratio.   *(2½ marks)*

(Total 35 marks)

QUESTION 63

You are required to produce an amended trial balance at 31.12.1985 for Burlingame Ltd from the following list of balances and notes after making the necessary Journal Entries.

(20 marks)

List of balances at 31.12.1985

	£
Land and Buildings at cost	72,000
Motor Vehicles at cost	10,000
Stock at 1.1.85	6,250
Debtors	5,150
Bank	2,750
Cash	100
Purchases	19,650
Drawings	7,000
Carriage Inwards	250
Returns Inwards	500
Returns Outwards	350
Discount Received	600
Discount Allowed	450
Wages and Salaries Expenses	2,500
Postage and Stationery Expenses	250
Rent and Rates Expenses	1,400
Light and Heat Expenses	1,250
Bad Debt Expenses	250
Sales	34,500
Creditors	6,350
Provisions for Depreciation	
Land and Buildings	20,000
Motor Vehicles	4,375
Provision for Bad Debts	200
Capital	60,000
Loan	3,375

Notes:

1. Stock at 31.12.85 £5,950.
2. The provision for bad debts is to be made equivalent to 1% of the annual sales figure.
3. Depreciation is to be provided as follows:—
   Land and Buildings 2% p.a. on cost.
   Motor Vehicles 25% p.a. on the reducing balance basis.
4. Rent and Rates in the list of balances includes a payment of £200 in respect of 1986.
5. Advertising expenditure amounting to £150 was incurred in December 1985 but had not been paid at 31st December 1985, although an invoice had been received but not entered through the books at the time the list of balances was extracted.

ANSWER 1

This question is designed to test knowledge of accounting principles and practices.

Comments should include:
Sales
Unless there is a very good reason for not so doing, credit sales should be included at the amount receivable; VAT should be excluded from the sales figure; cash discounts should be treated as an expense not as a deduction from revenue. — The Matching Principle (SSAP 2); VAT (SSAP 5).

Cost of sales
Opening and closing stocks should be valued on the same basis and the effect on profit of the change in policy should be stated. — Consistency (SSAP 2).

Purchases should be at catalogue price less trade discounts and excluding VAT (except for a few specialist transactions or circumstances).

Wages and salaries
These should be charged on the basis of amounts earned during the period, not the cash amounts paid. — The Matching Principle (SSAP 2).

Depreciation
It is quite in order for a business to employ different methods of calculating depreciation for different classes of fixed assets. Therefore, no note is needed. — Matters of Accounting Policy on Depreciation (SSAP 12).

General
If an unexplained difference arises on a balance sheet, the source(s) of the difference must be identified and the corrections made, using journals. Usually errors of understatement or overstatement for a particular account(s).

Goods used by owner are a drawing, not an expense. The basis of inclusion of fixed assets should be given.

ANSWER 2

This question is testing your knowledge of cut-off points.

Item	Reason for adjustment	Necessary Adjustment Increase £	Decrease £
(1)	No adjustment. Cost is lower than net realisable value (£800–£120)	—	—
(2)	Reduce to net realisable value (200 – (110 – 40))		130
(3)	Correction of arithmetical errors	72	
(4)	Items omitted in error	2,010	
(5)	Correction of transposition error		9
(6)	Goods omitted from stock count	638	
(7)	Elimination of hired item		347
(8)	Elimination of samples not for resale		63
(9)	Goods held by customers on a sale or return basis reduced to cost		184
(10)	Elimination of goods received not yet adopted		267
		2,720 (1,126)	1,126
	Net increase per adjustments	1,594	
	Add Stock at 31 May 1985: original	87,612	
	: amended stock at 31 May	£89,206	

ANSWER 3

Students should discuss the following points:—

Cash Accounting is often said to be the only objective measurement. Receipts and Payments are measured in objective terms and are not in any way subjective. However, once we attempt to measure profit by using the matching principle we immediately enter the realms of subjectivity.

The main subjective matters involved in drawing up financial statements in order to measure profitability are:—
1 How depreciation is to be charged (SSAP 12).
2 What Provisions are to be made? e.g. for Bad Debts.
3 How costs are matched with revenues.
4 Stock valuations and the inclusion of overheads (SSAP 9).

When charging depreciation we make subjective measures, regarding the method of depreciation we choose, the estimated useful life of the asset and any residual value.

A provision is defined in the Companies Act 1985 as 'an amount written off or retained to provide for a known liability, the amount of which cannot be ascertained with substantial accuracy.' Thus, subjectivity is even embodied in statute.

As accountants we should, however, attempt to be objective and try to follow the other principles stated in SSAP 2 apart from that of the accrual concept, i.e. Prudence and consistency.

ANSWER 4

1. (a) Capital Expenditure — Expenditure/investment in assets which will remain in the business earning revenue over a number of years. The charge for the use of the asset being by means of a depreciation expense as it is used up (the Matching Principle).

(b) (a), (b) and (e) regarded as Capital Expenditure for the reason explained in (a). Students expected to give detail for each of (a) to (e).

2. Original Profit £10,100

Less Expenses:
Repairs to typewriters (c)	500	
Delivery van (d)	500	
Depreciation:		
Buildings (a) and (e)	512.50	
Office equipment (b)	62.50	
		(1,575)

REVISED ESTIMATED PROFIT £ 8,525

ANSWER 5

1. The student would be expected to discuss the following points.

1. 'Profit is not cash' should be explained by the student briefly discussing the Accrual Concept (Matching Principle). Mention might be made of non-cash expenses such as Depreciation, Bad Debts, Accrued Expenses and Prepayments. A good student would mention the fact that this concept attempts to match the expenses of a period with the revenue earned in that same period. Differences between Capital and Revenue Expenditure.

2. Depreciation is the charge for use (or by time) of an asset. It attempts to use the matching principle by allocating the charge for the use of an Asset over its useful life. It would be misleading to charge the capital cost of an asset (which would last over a number of years during which it could be earning revenue) against only one year's revenue.

3. Just a brief discussion of the following would suffice:— The value of the business is essentially its value in exchange, i.e. what someone else is prepared to pay for it. The Balance Sheet Value is based on the Historic Cost Concept, i.e. what the business paid for the assets etc. Thus, if buildings were shown in the Balance Sheet at a N.B.V. of zero but a cost of £10,000 this would almost certainly not be their value today. They could be worth £100,000.

4. In the short term it is important that a business has sufficient cash or near liquid funds to pay its debts. A brief discussion of the Working Capital concept explaining the importance of working capital, the idea that a firm is able to meet its current liabilities out of its current assets. A good student might mention the usefulness of cash flow statements as a planning tool in this respect. Profitability is also important in the longer term to ensure the long term survival of the business. If a business is selling its product at below cost simply to generate cash to meet its short term liabilities, then in the longer term it will not survive because it would have insufficient funds from which to start the working capital cycle again. It would diminish in size. Furthermore, if a business is not earning sufficient profits, it would be better to cease trading and earn a higher rate of return by doing something else, e.g. investing in someone else's 'profitable' business.

5. Students should discuss briefly the need for financial statements to be consistent, e.g. for the financial statements to be meaningful. Charges such as depreciation need to be calculated on the same basis from period to period. Users are trying to determine the economic performance of the business unit over time. If statements are prepared on an inconsistent basis then this will diminish the usefulness of the reported figures and may give rise to misleading information.

All financial statements are drawn up on the going concern basis otherwise they would be prepared in line with the rules of liquidation. Students would be expected to state briefly what is meant by 'going concern', i.e. that the business was going to continue into the foreseeable future, rather than be discontinued and its various assets sold for what they could fetch.

ANSWER 6

The question requires a knowledge of the users and uses of accounting information.

Any 6 of the following types of individual/institution.

Employees	Ability to meet wage demands; Future prospects.
Shareholders (actual and potential)	Profit and profitability; Dividend paid and prospects for future through capital growth.
Customers	To ensure future suppliers.
Suppliers	Ability of company to pay its creditors.
Lenders	Ability of company to pay interest and to repay principal on due dates.
Government	Inland Revenue — Income and Corporation Tax; HM Customs & Excise — VAT; Department of Trade & Industry for government statistics.
Business Analysts	To predict share values for clients or for articles in Financial Press etc.; Long and short term strengths and weaknesses.
Competitors	Assessment of comparative performance and position.

Note: The Corporate Report published by the Accounting Standards Committee in 1975 outlined a number of users of Financial Statements. A summary may be found in a more detailed form in Hines — Basic Concepts in Foundation Accounting, published by Checkmate/Arnold 1986.

ANSWER 7

WORKING PAPER AS AT 31.12.84

$$\text{Provision Bad Debts} = 2\% \text{ of } 6250$$
$$= £125$$

Bad Debt Account

Bal b/f	150	Bal c/f to p/l	225
Provision	75		
	£225		£225

Provision Bad Debt Account

Bal c/f	125	Bal b/f	50
		Bad Debt a/c	75
	£125		£125

Advertising Ex. Account

Bal b/f	2,100	Bal c/f to p/l	2,350
Accrual	250		
	£2,350		£2,350

Accrual Account

Bal c/f	250	Advertising	250
	£250		£250

Secretarial Account

Bal b/f	1,500	Prepayment	100
		Bal c/f to p/l	1,400
	£1,500		£1,500

Prepayment Account

Secretarial	100	Bal c/f	100
	£100		£100

M.V. Depreciation Account

Provision	3,000	Bal c/f to p/l	3,000
	£3,000		£3,000

M.V. Provision Depreciation Account

Bal c/f	9,000	Bal b/f	6,000
		Depreciation P/L	3,000
	£9,000		£9,000

Mach. Depreciation Account

Provision	840	Bal c/f to p/l	840
	£840		£840

Mach. Provision Depreciation Account

Bal c/f	4,440	Bal b/f	3,600
		Depreciation P/L	840
	£4,440		£4,440

L & B Depreciation Account

Provision	1,000	Bal c/f to p/l	1,000
	£1,000		£1,000

L & B Provision Depreciation Account

Bal c/f	26,000	Bal b/f	25,000
		Depreciation P/L	1,000
	£26,000		£26,000

JOHNNY BARROW TRADING, PROFIT & LOSS ACCOUNT for period ended 31.12.84

SALES		35,500
LESS COST OF SALES		
Opening Stock	7,500	
Add Purchases	25,000	
	32,500	
Less Closing stock	5,350	
		27,150
GROSS PROFIT		£8,350
LESS EXPENSES		
Secretarial	1,400	
Wages	3,000	
Advertising	2,350	
Bad Debts	225	
Discount Allowed	50	
Depreciation	4,840	
		11,865
NET PROFIT/(LOSS)		(3,515)

JOHNNY BARROW BALANCE SHEET as at 31.12.84

FIXED ASSETS	£Cost	£Depn.	£NBV
Motor Vehicle	15,000	9,000	6,000
Machinery	12,000	4,440	7,560
Land & Buildings	50,000	26,000	24,000
	£77,000	£39,440	37,560

CURRENT ASSETS			
Stock		5,350	
Debtors	6,250		
Less Provision	125		
		6,125	
Bank		1,250	
Cash		500	
Prepayments		100	
			13,325

LESS CURRENT LIABILITIES			
Creditors		5,250	
Accruals		250	
		5,500	
Net Current Assets			7,825
Total Net Assets			£45,385

FINANCED BY:

Capital	50,000	
Less Loss	(3,515)	
	46,485	
Less Drawings	(1,500)	
		44,985
Add Loan — Van Hire		400
CAPITAL EMPLOYED		45,385

ANSWER 8

Trading and Profit & Loss Account for period ended 30.6.84

	£Dr	£Cr
Sales		10,000
Less Cost of Sales		
Purchases	10,150	
+ Opening Stock 1.7.83	3,250	
	13,400	
– Closing Stock 30.6.84	(5,000)	
		(8,400)
Gross Profit		£1,600
Less Expenses		
Advertising	280	
Rent	100	
Rates	120	
Administration	600	
Distribution	170	
		1,170
Net Profit/(Loss)		£ 430

Fred's Balance Sheet as at 30.6.84

	£Cost	£Depn.	£NBV
Fixed Assets			
Premises	10,000		10,000
Motor vehicle	5,500		5,500
Machinery	3,500		3,500
	19,000	—	19,000
Current Assets			
Stock	5,000		
Debtors	4,100		
Prepayment	30		
Cash	600		
		9,830	
Less Current Liabilities			
Creditors	3,320		
Accruals	80		
		(3,400)	
Net Current Assets (Working Capital)			6,430
Total Net Assets			25,430
Financed By			
Capital		20,000	
Add Retained Profit		430	
		20,430	
Loan		5,000	
Capital Employed			25,430

Working Paper

Rates Exp. A/c

	£Dr		£Cr
Balance b/f	150	Prepayments	30
		Balance c/f P/L	120
	150		150

Prepayments A/c

Rates	30	Balance c/f	30
	30		30

Advertising Ex. A/c

Balance b/f	250		
Accrual	30	Balance c/f P/L	280
	280		280

Distribution Ex. A/c

Balance b/f	120		
Accrual	50	Balance c/f P/L	170
	170		170

Accruals A/c

		Advertising	30
Balance c/f	80	Distribution	50
	80		80

ANSWER 9

WORKING PAPER AT 31.12.84

SALES ACCOUNT (Revenue)

	£Dr		£Cr
Balance c/f to Trading A/c	31,000	Balance b/f	30,000
		Debtors	1,000
	£31,000		£31,000

DEBTORS ACCOUNT (Asset)

	£Dr		£Cr
Balance b/f	6,250	Balance c/f	7,250
Sales	1,000		
	£7,250		£7,250

Provision for bad debts calculated as follows:—

Closing debtors figure	=	£7,250
Bad debts	=	£7,250 x 5%
Bad debts	=	£362.50

BAD DEBT PROVISION ACCOUNT (Liability)

	£Dr		£Cr
Balance c/f	362.50	Balance b/f	200.00
		Bad debts	162.50
	362.50		362.50

BAD DEBTS ACCOUNT (Expense)

	£Dr		£Cr
Balance b/f	100.00	Balance c/f	262.50
Provision	162.50		
	262.50		262.50

INTEREST ON LOAN ACCOUNT (Expense)

	£457		£457
Bank	£457	Balance c/f	£457

Interest calculated 10% of £4,570.

BANK ACCOUNT (Asset)

	£Dr		£Cr
Balance b/f	2,500	Interest on loan	457
		Balance c/f	2,043
	£2,500		£2,500

RENT ACCOUNT (Expense)

	£Dr		£Cr
Balance b/f	2,600	Prepayment	200
		Balance c/f	2,400
	£2,600		£2,600

ACCOMMODATION ACCOUNT (Expense)

	£Dr		£Cr
Balance b/f	250	Balance c/f	400
Accrual	150		
	£400		£400

PREPAYMENT ACCOUNT (Asset)

	£Dr		£Cr
Rent	£200	Balance c/f	£200

ACCRUAL ACCOUNT (Liability)

	£Dr		£Cr
Balance c/f	£150	Accommodation	£150

Depreciation calculated as follows:
1) Land and Buildings £50,000 ÷ 50 years = £1,000 p.a.
2) Motor Vehicle £15,000 − £5,400 = £9,600
   £9,600 x 20% = £1,920 depreciation
   for this year

H. LAMAR TRADING, PROFIT & LOSS A/C FOR PERIOD ENDED 31.12.84

	£	£	£
SALES TURNOVER			31,000
Less Returns inwards			(500)
			30,500
LESS COST OF SALES			
Opening stock 1.1.84		7,500	
Add purchases	21,500		
Less Returns outwards	(1,000)		
		20,500	
		28,000	
Less stock 31.12.84		(4,750)	
			23,250
GROSS PROFIT			£7,250
Less Expenses			
Advertising		2,500	
Rent		2,400	
Light and heat		550	
Motor Vehicle running		1,120	
Accommodation		400	
Bad debts		262.50	
Depreciation		2,920	
Interest on loan		457	
			(10,609.50)
NET PROFIT/(LOSS)			(£3,359.50)

H. LAMAR BALANCE SHEET AS AT 31.12.84

FIXED ASSETS		Cost £	Provision for Depn. £	NBV £
Land and Buildings		50,000	16,000	34,000
Motor Vehicle		15,000	7,320	7,680
		65,000	23,320	41,680

CURRENT ASSETS

Stock		4,750	
Debtors	7,250		
Less Bad debt provision	362.50	6,887.50	
Prepayments		200	
Bank		2,043	
Cash		300	
			14,180.50

LESS CURRENT LIABILITIES

Creditors	5,500	
Accruals	150	
		5,650

NET CURRENT ASSETS	8,530.50
TOTAL NET ASSETS (NET WORTH)	£50,210.50

FINANCED BY

Capital	50,000	
Less drawings	1,000	
	49,000	
Add retained profit/(loss)	(3,359.50)	
	45,640.50	
Add loan	4,570	
CAPITAL EMPLOYED		£50,210.50

ANSWER 10

CAPITAL ACCOUNT

	Acc. Name	£Dr			Acc. Name	£Cr
				Jan. 1	Cash	6000
Mar. 31	Balance c/f	6000				
		6000				6000
				Apr. 1	Balance b/f	6000

CREDITORS ACCOUNT

					Acc. Name	
				Feb.	Stock	3000
				Feb.	Entertain- ing Clients	150
				Feb.	Advertising	50
Mar. 31	Balance c/f	3200				
		3200				3200
				Apr. 1	Balance b/f	3200

LOAN ACCOUNT

				Jan. 1	Cash	3000
Mar. 31	Balance c/f	3000				
		3000				3000
				Apr. 1	Balance b/f	3000

CASH ACCOUNT

Jan.	Capital	6000		Jan.	Delivery Van	2000
Jan.	Loan	3000		Jan.	Premises	4000
				Jan.	Buying Trips	750
				Mar. 31	Balance c/f	2250
		9000				9000
Apr. 1	Balance b/f	2250				

FIXED ASSETS DELIVERY VAN

Jan.	Cash	2000	Mar. 31	Balance c/f	2000
Apr. 1	Balance b/f	2000			

FIXED ASSETS PREMISES

Jan.	Cash	4000	Mar. 31	Balance c/f	4000
		4000			4000
Apr. 1	Balance b/f	4000			

STOCK ACCOUNT

Feb.	Creditor	3000	Feb.	Cost of Sales	1850
			Mar. 31	Balance c/f	1150
		3000			3000
Apr. 1	Balance b/f	1150			

BUYING TRIPS EXPENSE ACCOUNT

Feb.	Cash	750	Mar. 31	Balance c/f	750
		750			750
Apr. 1	Balance b/f	750			

ENTERTAINING CLIENTS EXPENSE ACCOUNT

Feb.	Creditor	150	Mar. 31	Balance c/f	150
		150			150
Apr. 1	Balance b/f	150			

ADVERTISING EXPENSE ACCOUNT

Feb.	Creditor	50				
			Mar. 31	Balance c/f	50	
		50			50	
Apr. 1	Balance b/f	50				

SALES ACCOUNT

			Feb.	Debtor	2500	
Mar. 31	Balance c/f	2500				
		2500			2500	
			Apr. 1	Balance b/f	2500	

DEBTORS ACCOUNT

Feb.	Sales	2500				
			Mar. 31	Balance c/f	2500	
		2500			2500	
Apr. 1	Balance b/f	2500				

COST OF SALES ACCOUNT

Feb.	Stock	1850				
			Mar. 31	Balance c/f	1850	
		1850			1850	
Apr. 1	Balance b/f	1850				

ROD — TRIAL BALANCE for period ended 31st March 1984

	£Dr	£Cr
Capital		6000
Creditors		3200
Loan		3000
Cash	2250	
Delivery Van	2000	
Premises	4000	
Stock	1150	
Buying Trips	750	
Entertaining Clients	150	
Advertising	50	
Sales		2500
Debtors	2500	
Cost of Sales	1850	
	14700	14700

ROD — TRADING AND PROFIT AND LOSS A/C for period ended 31st March 1984

	£	£
Sales		2500
Less Cost of Sales		
Opening Stock	NIL	
Add Purchases	3000	
	3000	
Less Closing Stock	(1150)	
		(1850)
Gross Profit		650
Less Expenses		
Buying Trips	750	
Entertaining clients	150	
Advertising	50	
		(950)
Net Profit/(Loss)		(300)

ROD — BALANCE SHEET as at 31st March 1984

	£Cost	£Depn.	£NBV
Fixed Assets			
Delivery Van	2000	—	2000
Premises	4000	—	4000
	6000	—	6000
Current Assets			
Stock	1150		
Debtors	2500		
Cash	2250		
		5900	
Current Liabilities	3200	(3200)	
			2700
			8700
Financed By			
Capital		6000	
Net Profit/(Loss)		(300)	
			5700
Loan			3000
Capital Employed			8700

(1) $\dfrac{650}{2500} = 26\%$ $\qquad \dfrac{(300)}{2500} = -12\%$

He made a 26% gross profit but his expenses are too much for him to afford.

ANSWER 11

MICKY — Trading, Profit & Loss Account
for the year ending 31.12.85

	£	£
Sales		50,000
Less Returns Inwards		(250)
Net Sales		49,750
Less Cost of Sales		
Opening Stock	4,750	
Add Purchases	22,000	
Carriage Inwards	150	
	26,900	
Less Returns Outwards	(500)	
	26,400	
Less Closing Stock	(4,750)	
Cost of Sales		21,650
Gross Profit		28,100
Add Non-Trading Income		
Discount Received		700
		28,800
Less Expenses		
Carriage Outwards	200	
Wages & Salaries	5,100	
Advertising	2,200	
Travelling	1,000	
Accommodation	500	
Rent (900 + 300)	1,200	
Rates (300 + 990)	1,290	
Postage & Stationery	101	
Light & Heat	2,250	
Depreciation:		
Land & Buildings	2,000	
Plant & Machinery	2,025	
Motor Vehicles	2,000	
Discount Allowed	450	(20,316)
Net Profit		8,484

MICKY — Balance Sheet at 31.12.85

Fixed Assets	£ Cost	£ Provision for Depreciation	£ Net Book Value
Land & Buildings	100,000	42,000	58,000
Motor Vehicles	10,000	6,000	4,000
Plant & Machinery	25,000	6,775	18,225
	135,000	54,775	80,225

Current Assets

Stock	4,750		
Debtors	5,250		
Prepayments	49		
Bank	3,200		
Cash	1,000		
		14,249	

Less Current Liabilities

Creditors	4,800		
Accruals	1,290		
		(6,090)	

Net Current Assets			8,159
Total Net Assets			88,384

Financed by

Capital	80,000		
Net Profit Retained	8,484		
	88,484		
Drawings	(4,100)		
Total Equity	84,384		

Long Term Liabilities

Loan	4,000		
Capital Employed			88,384

ANSWER 12

3.(a)   MID-CHESHIRE CRICKET CLUB
Computation of capital on 1 January 1984

	£	£
Equipment and machinery		160
Cash in hand		20
Balances at bank — Deposit account	446	
— Current account (1)	60	
		506
Subscriptions due		30
		716
Less: Sums due for printing and secretarial expenses	20	
Honoraria to secretary and treasurer	80	
		100
Accumulated fund on 1 January 1984		616

(5 marks)

3.(b)   Income and Expenditure Account
for the year ended 31 December 1984

	£		£	£
Groundsman's fees	150	Donations and		
Rent of grounds	50	subscriptions (3)		510
Fares less contribution (80-20)	60	Receipts from teas	60	
Printing and secretarial expenses (2)	52	Less: Cost of teas	50	
Repairs (5)	90			10
Honoraria	120	Net proceeds of dance		156
Groundsman's bonus	40	Bank interest		10
Loss on sale of equipment	94			
Excess of income over expenditure	30			
	686			686

(10 marks)

Mid-Cheshire Cricket Club
Balance Sheet at 31.12.84

	£	£
Fixed assets		
Machinery and equipment (4)		350
Current assets		
Debtors — subscriptions	20	
Balances at bank and cash in hand	452	
	472	
Less: Current liabilities		
Sundry creditors (6)	176	
		296
		646
Financed by		
Accumulated fund		
1 January 1984		616
Excess of income over expenditure for the year		30
		646

(5 marks)

WORKINGS

(1) Balances at bank — current account

	£
1 January 1984	120
Less: Unpresented cheque	60
	60
31 December 1984	30
Less: Unpresented cheque	50
	20 o/d

(2) Printing and secretarial expenses

		£			£
31 Dec.	Cash	56	1 Jan.	Balance b/f	20
	Balance c/f	16	31 Dec.	Income and expenditure a/c	52
		72			72

(3) Donations and subscriptions

		£			£
1 Jan.	Balance b/f	30	31 Dec.	Cash	520
31 Dec.	I & E a/c	510		Balance c/f	20
		540			540

(4) Machinery and equipment account

	£			£
1 Jan. Balance b/f	160	31 Dec. CB — Sale of		
31 Dec. Cash Book	300	equipment		16
		I & E a/c —		
		depreciation		
		(loss on sale)		94
		Balance c/f		350
	460			460

(5) Repairs

	£			£
31 Dec. Cash	100	1 Jan. Balance b/f		60
Balance c/f	50	31 Dec. I & E a/c		90
	150			150

(6) Creditors

	£
Printing and secretarial	16
Honoraria	120
Groundsman's bonus	40
	176

ANSWER 13

WCC Statement of Affairs at 1.1.83

			NBV £
Fixed Assets			
Land			8,000
Clubhouse			4,000
Equipment			1,100
			13,100
Current Assets			
Bar Stock	992		
Debtors (Subscriptions)	110		
Cash	1048	2,150	
Less Current Liabilities			
Creditors (588 + 50)		638	
Net Current Assets			1,512
			14,612
Financed by			
Accumulated Fund			14,612

WCC Bar Trading Account for year ended 31.12.83

	£	£
Bar Sales		11.256
Less Cost of Sales		
Opening Stock	992	
+ Purchases (1)	8,016	
	9,008	
– Closing Stock	1,116	(7,892)
Gross Profit		3,364
Less Expenses		
Wages	1,248	
Bar Expenses (2)	488	(1,736)
NET PROFIT		1,628

Workings:—

(1) Bar Purchase Control Account

Cash	7924	Balance b/f	588
Balance c/f	680	Bar Trading	8016
	8604		8604

(2) Bar Expenses Account

Cash	468	Balance b/f	50
Balance c/f	70	Bar Trading a/c	488
	538		538

WCC Income and Expenditure Account
for year ended 31.12.83

	£	£
INCOME		
Subscription (1)		2,604
Profit on Bar		1,628
Donations		240
		4,472
EXPENDITURE		
Wages — Groundsman	1,878	
Repairs to Clubhouse	238	
Ground Upkeep	458	
Secretary	276	
Coach Hire (2)	675	

Depreciation — Clubhouse	400		
— Equipment	220	620	(4,145)
Surplus of Income over Expenditure			327

Workings:—

(1) Subscriptions Account

Balance b/f	110	Cash	2,662
I & E Account	2,604	Balance c/f	132
Accruals in respect	80		
of 1984 Subs.			
	2,794		2,794

(2) Coach Hire

Cash	610	I & E	675
Balance c/f	65		
	675		675

WCC Statement of Affairs at 31.12.83

	£ Value at 1.1	£ Provision for Depreciation	£ Net Book Value
Fixed Assets			
Land	8,000	—	8,000
Clubhouse	4,000	400	3,600
Equipment	1,100	220	880
	13,100	620	12,480
Current Assets			
Bar Stocks	1,116		
Debtors Subscription	132		
Prepayments	—		
Bank & Cash	2,106		
		3,354	
Less Current Liabilities			
Trade Creditors	680		
Other Creditors (70 + 65)	135		
Accruals — Members paid for 1984	80		
		(895)	
NET CURRENT ASSETS			2,459
TOTAL NET ASSETS			14,939
FINANCED BY:			
Accumulated Fund a 1.1.83	14,612		
Add Surplus of Income over Expenditure	327		
Accumulated fund a 31.12.83			14,939

2.(i) An Income and Expenditure Account supported by Balance Sheets at 1.1.83 and 31.12.83 would be more appropriate since this attempts to match expenses of the period with the income of the period. Most non-profit making organisations such as charities, clubs and societies use this type of financial statement. It gives members a more meaningful picture of the club's affairs over the time period in question.

ANSWER 14

Manufacturing, Trading and Profit and Loss A/c of Jones Ltd. for the year ended 30.4.82

		£	£
	Transferred Finished Goods to Trading Account		337,000
	Cost of Manufacture		
	Cost of Materials used:		
	Stock of R.M. 1.5.81	45,000	
	Add Purchases	154,000	
		199,000	
	Less: Stock of R.M. 30.4.82	49,000	
A	**Cost of Raw Materials Consumed**	150,000	
	DIRECT COSTS		
	Manufacturing Wages	80,000	
	Power	15,000	
B	**PRIME COST OF PRODUCTION**	245,000	
	FACTORY OVERHEADS		
	Manufacturing Expenses	30,300	
	Repairs & Maintenance	18,500	
	Factory Depreciation	40,000	
	Light & Heat	5,400	
		94,200	
		339,200	
	CHANGE IN WIP STOCK		
	Add WIP (1.5.81)	21,000	
	Less WIP (30.4.82)	23,200	
		(2,200)	
C	Cost of Finished Goods at Factory	337,000	337,000

		£	£
Sales			500,000
Less Cost of Sales			
Stock of FG at 1.5.81		60,000	
Add Purchases of FG		11,000	
		71,000	
Add FG Produced at Cost		337,000	
		408,000	
Less Finished Goods at 30.4		68,000	
D Cost of FG Sold			340,000
E **Gross Profit**			160,000

Less Expenses			
Administration			
Depreciation	8,000		
Light & Heat	800		
Admin. Expenses	22,200		
		31,000	
Selling and Distribution			
Depreciation	9,000		
Light & Heat	3,300		
Carriage Out	6,600		
Expenses	31,100		
		50,000	
			(81,000)
F **NET PROFIT**			79,000

ANSWER 15

Summers Ltd. Manufacturing & Trading and Profit and Loss Account for the year ended 31.3.84

	£	£
Factory Cost of Production transferred to the Trading Account		63,661
Direct Materials		
Opening Stock R.M.	7,102	
Purchases	49,944	
	57,046	
Less Closing Stock R.M.	(7,064)	
Raw Materials consumed	49,982	
Direct Labour		
Manufacturing wages	10,054	
PRIME COST	60,036	
Factory Overheads		
Light & heat	1,445	
Sundry Expenses	530	
Depreciation Plant	500	
Rent & Rates	150	
		2,625
Change in WIP Stock		
Add O/S	3,500	
Less Closing Stock	(2,500)	
		1,000
		63,661	63,661
Sales		71,580
Less Cost of Sales		
O/S F.G.	7,278	
Add Factory Cost of Prodn.	63,661	
	70,939	
Less C/S F.G.	7,448	
		63,491
Gross Profit		8,089
Less Expenses		
Administrative		
Light & Heat	138	
Office Salaries	2,116	
Sundry Office Exp.	399	
Depn. Office Machinery	100	
Rent & Rates Office	69	
	2,822	

Sales Marketing Distribution

Advertising	808	
Salesman's commission	880	
Bad Debt Provision	303	
		1,991
Total Overheads		4,813
Net Profit Retained		3,276

Summers Ltd. Balance Sheet as at 31.3.84

	£ Cost	£ Depn.	£ N.B.V.
Fixed Assets			
Premises	4,050	—	4,050
Plant	10,000	3,000	7,000
Office Machinery	1,000	600	400
	15,050	3,600	11,450
Current Assets			
Stock Raw Material	7,064		
WIP	7,448		
F.G.	2,500		
Debtors (7575-303)	7,272		
Prepayments	48		
Bank & Cash	2,013		
		26,345	
Less Current Liabilities			
Trade Creditors	7,733		
Accruals	136		
		7,869	
Net Current Assets (Working Capital)			18,476
TOTAL NET ASSETS			29,926
Financed by			
Capital	22,650		
Net Profit Retained	3,276		
	25,926		
Less Drawings	(1,600)		
Capital Employed			29,926

ANSWER 16

Dalglish & Rush Trading and Profit and Loss
Appropriation Account for the year ended 31.12.83

	£	£
Sales		24,000
Less Returns in		(200)
		23,800
Less Cost of Sales		
1.1 Stock	2,500	
Purchases	16,000	
	18,500	
31.12 Stock	2,800	15,700
Gross Profit		8,100
Less Expenses		
Bad debts	200	
Wages (4,000 + 500)	4,500	
Advertising	3,000	
Insurance	1,000	
Sundry Expenses	500	
Discount Allowed	300	
Depreciation		
Premises 10% 400		
Fixtures 20% 400	800	
		10,300
Net Profit/(Loss)		(2,200)
Interest on Capital:		
Dalglish	500	
Rush	300	
		(800)
		(3,000)
Balance of Losses:		
Dalglish	(1,800)	
Rush	(1,200)	
		(3,000)

Dalglish Current Account for year ended 31.12.83

	£	£
Balance b/f		2,000
Add Interest on Capital		500
Less share of loss	1,800	
Less Drawings	3,000	
		4,800
Balance c/f		(2,300)

Rush Current Account for year ended 31.12.83

	£	£
Balance b/f		1,000
Add Interest on Capital		300
Less share of loss	1,200	
Less Drawings	2,500	
		3,700
Balance c/f		(2,400)

Dalglish & Rush Balance Sheet as at 31.12.83

	Cost £	Depn. £	NBV £
Fixed Assets			
Premises	4,000	400	3,600
Fixtures	2,000	400	1,600
	6,000	800	5,200
Current Assets			
Stock	2,800		
Debtors	6,000		
Cash	800		
		9,600	
Less Current Liabilities			
Creditors	3,000		
Accruals	500	3,500	
Net Current Assets			6,100
Net Worth			11,300

Financed by

CAPITAL ACCOUNTS

Dalglish	10,000	
Rush	6,000	
		16,000

CURRENT ACCOUNTS

Dalglish	(2,300)	
Rush	(2,400)	
		(4,700)
Capital Employed		11,300

Students should briefly discuss the following points:—

1. Set up a Realization Account and transfer all provisions, assets sold, assets taken by partners for their own use, Dissolution Costs and Proceeds from sale.
2. Discharge all liabilities of the partnership, if need be by partners making up any deficiencies on their Capital account from their own funds.
3. Transfer balances on Partners Current accounts to their Capital accounts.
4. Share profits or losses in their partnership profit sharing ratios.
5. Cash available should be equal to credit balances on capital accounts provided any partner in debit has been able to pay in the amount due from him.

ANSWER 17

DUM & DEE Profit and Loss and Appropriation A/c
for the year ended 31.12.85

	£	£
Sales		51,550
LESS Cost of Sales		
Opening Stock	5,550	
Add Purchases	29,525	
Carriage Inward	100	
	35,175	
Less Closing Stock	(5,385)	
		(29,790)
GROSS PROFIT		21,760
Add Non-Trading Income: Discount Received		300
		22,060
Less Expenses		
Administration		
Wages & Salaries	7,500	
Office Repairs	500	
Telephone	350	
Rent & Rates Office (1800—600P)	1,200	
Land & Buildings Depreciation		
(2% x £100,000)	2,000	
Sales and Marketing		
Advertising (2750 + 750A)	3,500	
Salesman's Salary	8,000	
Vehicle Running	2,150	
Vehicle Depreciation		
(25% x 20% x 20,000)	1,000	
Discount Allowed	1,000	
Distribution		
Vehicle Running	4,250	
Repairs	1,100	
Depreciation (75% x 20% x 20,000)	3,000	
Carriage Outwards	1,000	
Finance		
Bank Charges	550	
		(37,100)
Net Loss (before appropriation)		(15,040)
Add: Interest on Drawings — Dum		120
— Dee		50
		(14,870)

LESS: Interest on Capitals

	— Dum	2,500	
	— Dee	2,000	
Salary	— Dee	5,000	
			(9,500)

Total Net Loss (after appropriation)		(24,370)
Shared as follows:—		
Dum (50%)	12,185	
Dee (50%)	12,185	
		(24,370)

PARTNERS' CURRENT ACCOUNTS
DUM — Current Account

	£Dr		£Cr
Interest on Drawings	120	Balance b/f	8,185
Bank — Drawings	1,200	Interest on Capital	2,500
Share of Loss ½	12,185	Balance c/f	2,820
	13,505		13,505

DEE — Current Account

	£Dr		£Cr
Interest on Drawings	50	Balance b/f	4,400
Bank — Drawings	500	Interest on Capital	2,000
Share of Loss ½	12,185	Salary	5,000
		Balance c/f	1,335
	12,735		12,735

DUM & DEE — Balance Sheet at 31.12.1985

	£ Cost	£ Provision for Depreciation	£ Net Book Value
Fixed Assets			
Land & Buildings	100,000	32,000	68,000
Motor Vehicles	20,000	9,000	11,000
	120,000	41,000	79,000
Current Assets			
Stock	5,385		
Debtors	7,250		
Prepayments	600		
Bank (3200 – 1700 Drawing)	1,500		
Cash	510		
		15,245	
Less Current Liabilities			
Creditors	7,650		
Accruals	750		
		(8,400)	
Net Current Assets — WORKING CAPITAL			6,845
TOTAL NET ASSETS — NET WORTH			85,845
Financed by:			
Capitals — DUM	50,000		
— DEE	40,000		
		90,000	
Current Accounts			
— DUM	(2,820)		
— DEE	(1,325)		
		(4,155)	
CAPITAL EMPLOYED			85,845

ANSWER 18

Hot Rod Records Realisation Account

	£Dr		£Cr
Lease	14,000	Bank (Assets sold	
Fixtures and Fittings	1,200	for cash)	74,200
Motor van	1,100	Neil (Current a/c	
Stock	17,000	re van)	1,260
Debtors	15,200		
Balance: (Profit on realisation)			
Keith 1/4	6,740		
Tony 1/4	6,740		
Neil 1/4	6,740		
Geoff 1/4	6,740		
	26,960		
	75,460		75,460

(8 marks)

CASH BOOK

	£Dr			£Cr
Balance (per		Creditors		7,800
Balance Sheet)	6,400	**Partners' Current Accounts**		
Realisation Account	74,200	Keith	10,900	
		Tony	11,660	
		Neil	9,720	
		Geoff	10,520	
				42,800
		Partners' Capital Accounts		
		Keith	12,000	
		Tony	8,000	
		Neil	6,000	
		Geoff	4,000	
				30,000
	80,600			80,600

(4 marks)

PARTNERS' CURRENT ACCOUNTS

	Keith £	Tony £	Neil £	Geoff £		Keith £	Tony £	Neil £	Geoff £
Realisation A/c Motor Van			1,260		Balance per B/Sheet	4,160	4,920	4,240	3,780
Cash Book	10,900	11,660	9,720	10,520	Realisation A/c Profit	6,740	6,740	6,740	6,740
	10,900	11,660	10,980	10,520		10,900	11,660	10,980	10,520

(4 marks)

PARTNERS' CAPITAL ACCOUNTS

	Keith £	Tony £	Neil £	Geoff £		Keith £	Tony £	Neil £	Geoff £
Cash Book	12,000	8,000	6,000	4,000	Balance per Balance Sheet	12,000	8,000	6,000	4,000

(4 marks)

ANSWER 19

(a)

Sales Ledger Control Account

	£		£
Balance b/f	7,504	Returns inward	812
Cheques dishonoured	50	Cheques	42,074
Credit sales	49,836	Cash	1,122
		Bad debts	86
		Contra with purchase ledger	252
		Balance c/f	13.044
	57,390		57,390
Balance b/f	13,044		

(10 marks)

(b)

Sales Ledger Control Account

	£		£
Balance b/f	13,044	Contra with purchase ledger (3)	40
Bad debt recovered (1)	60	Discounts (6)	70
Sales day book (2)	200	Balance c/f	13,194
	13,304		13,304
Balance b/f	13,194		

(6 marks)

(c)

List of balances per sales ledger

	£
Total per draft list	13,294
Less: Newton (credit balance) (4)	260
	13,034
Add: Lamb's balance (5)	160
Total per Sales Ledger Control Account	13,194

(4 marks)

ANSWER 20

Sales Ledger Control Account

		£Dr				£Cr
May	1 Balance b/f	7,632	May	1	Balance b/f	44
	31 Sales	14,180		31	Cash	208
	31 Cash refunded	74		31	Bank	12,478
	31 Cash; dis-			31	Bad Debts	612
	honoured			31	Discounts	
	cheques	58			allowed	596
	31 Balance c/f	80		31	Returns	
					inwards	328
				31	Balance c/f	7,758
		22,024				22,024

(b) Control Accounts are normally in the charge of a responsible officer who makes entries separately from the individual ledger accounts. They are therefore a check on the entries and may prevent error or fraud. Total accounts are useful to extract Trial Balances quickly. They are similar to the Trial Balance insofar as Errors of Omission, Commission, Principle, Compensation, Original Entry and Reversal will not necessarily be detected.

ANSWER 21

Debtors Account

		£Dr			£Cr
30.6.80	Balance b/f	20,000	30.6.81	Bad debt provision..	3,000
30.6.81	Sales	200,000		Cash	193,000
	Bad debt provision ...	1,000		Balance c/f	25,000
		221,000			221,000

Provision for Bad Debts Account

		£Dr			£Cr
30.6.81	Debtors—written off..	3,000	30.6.80	Balance b/f	1,000
30.6.81	Balance c/f..........	1,250	30.6.81	Debtors—recovered	1,000
			30.6.81	P & L account	2,250
		4,250			4,250

Lighting and Heating Account

		£Dr			£Cr
30.6.80	Coke stock b/f	630	30.6.80	Accrued electricity	
30.6.81	Coke purchases	8,000		b/f	920
	Paid for electricity....	6,000	30.6.81	P & L account	13,633
	Accrued electricity c/f	673		Coke stock c/f	750
		15,303			15,303

ANSWER 22

ZEE LTD.
Creditors Control Account
for January 1986

		£Dr			£Cr
	Returns Out	7,860	1.1.86	Balance b/f	105,650
	Discount Received	10,850		Purchases	115,675
	Bank	104,650			
	Cash	1,000			
31.1	Balance c/f	96,965			
		221,325			221,325

Balance to c/f at 31.1. is £96,965

ANSWER 23

WORKING PAPER

Administration Expense a/c

Balance b/f	2,000	Balance c/f	2,300
Accrual	250		
Suspense	50		
	2,300		2,300

Suspense Account

Sales & Marketing	550	Balance b/f	990
Purchases	490	Administration	50
	1,040		1,040

Sales Account

Balance c/f	35,500	Balance b/f	35,000
			500
	35,500		35,500

Debtors Account

Balance b/f	4,750	Balance c/f	5,250
Sales	500		
	5,250		5,250

THE JOURNAL

	£Dr	£Cr
Suspense		50
Administration	50	
Suspense	550	
Sales & Marketing		550
Suspense	490	
Purchases		490

Sales & Marketing Expense Account

Balance b/f	3,500	Suspense	550
		Balance c/f	2,950
	3,500		3,500

Purchases Account

Balance b/f	20,050	Suspense	490
		Balance c/f	19,560
	20,050		20,050

Closing Debtors = £5,250 x 2.5%

Provision B.D. = £131.25

Provision Bad Debts

Balance c/f	131.25	Balance b/f	50
		Bad debts	81.25
	131.25		131.25

Bad Debts

Balance b/f	150	Balance c/f	231.25
Provision	81.25		
	231.25		231.25

Rent Account

Balance b/f	3,200	Prepayment	200
		Balance c/f	3,000
	3,200		3,200

Prepayment Account

Balance b/f	200	Balance c/f	400
Rent	200		
	400		400

Accrual Account

Balance c/f	350	Balance b/f	100
		Administration	250
	350		350

Depreciation calculated as follows:

L & B $\quad=\quad$ 100,000 – 50 years $\quad=$ 2,000 p.a.

Machinery $\quad=\quad$ 50,000 – 18,000 $\quad=\quad$ 32,000 x 20%

$\qquad\qquad=\quad$ 6,400 p.a.

M.V. $\qquad=\quad$ 20,000 x 20% $\quad=$ 4,000 p.a.

Repaid loan $\quad=$ **£3,000**

Interest on loan to be charged

19,180 x 10% $\quad=\quad$ 1918

Loan Account

Bank	3,000	Balance b/f	19,180
Balance c/f	16,180		
	19,180		19,180

Bank Account

Balance b/f	3,100	Loan	3,000
		Balance c/f	100
	100		100

D. Hoffman
Trading and Profit and Loss Account
for period ended 31.12.84

	£	£
Sales		35,500
Less Returns in		(150)
		35,350
Less Cost of Sales		
Stock 1.1	3,500	
Add Purchases	19,560	
	23,060	
Less Returns Out	(130)	
	22,930	
Less stock 31.12.84	(5,150)	
		(17,780)
GROSS PROFIT		17,570
Less Expenses		
Administration	2,300	
Sales & Marketing	2,950	
Rent	3,000	
Bad Debts	231.25	
Depreciation	12,400	
Interest on loan	1,918	
		22,799.25
NET PROFIT / (LOSS)		(5,229.25)

D. Hoffman
Balance Sheet as at 31.12.84

Fixed Assets	£Cost	£Depn.	£NBV
Land & Buildings	100,000	27,000	73,000
Machinery	50,000	24,400	25,600
Motor Vehicle	20,000	12,000	8,000
	170,000	63,400	106,600

Current Assets

Stock		5,150	
Debtors	5,250		
Less Provision	131.25		
		5,118.75	
Prepayments		400	
Bank		100	
Cash		100	
			10,868.75

Less Current Liabilities

Creditors	4,250		
Accruals	2,268		
		6,518	
Working Capital			4,350.75
NET WORTH			110,950.75

Financed by

Capital		100,000
Less Loss ꞁed Profit		(5,229.25)
		94,770.75
Add loan		16,180
CAPITAL EMPLOYED		110,950.75

ANSWER 24

EDGEWORTH JOURNAL

KEY TO QUESTION			£Dr	£Cr	Effect on Profit
Note: 1	1)	Motor Van	3,500		+3,500
		Motor Vehicle Expenses		3,500	
2	2)	Motor Vehicle Repairs	750		− 750
		Motor Vehicle		750	
4	3)	Land & Buildings	500		+ 500
		Legal Costs		500	
1	4)	Motor Vehicle Depreciation	700		− 700
		Provision Depreciation		700	
2	5)	Provision Depreciation M.V.	150		+ 150
		Depreciation Motor Vehicle		150	
5	6)	Land & buildings Depreciation	10		− 10
		Provision Depreciation		10	

KEY TO QUESTION	REVISED INCOME STATEMENT	£
1	Original Net Profit	7,600
	Add Motor Vehicle Expenses	3,500
		11,100
2	Less Motor Vehicle Repair	750
		10,350
4	Add Land & Buildings (Legal Costs)	500
		10,850
5	Less Depreciation Provision Motor Vehicle	700
		10,150
2	Add Provision for Depreciation Motor Vehicle	150
		10,300
3	Less Land & Buildings Depreciation	100
	REVISED NET PROFIT	**£10,200**

ANSWER 25

(a)

JOURNALS TO CORRECT

	Account Name	£Dr	£Cr	Effect on Profit +	Effect on Profit −	Effect on Capital Employed +	Effect on Capital Employed −
1	Discount Allowed	536			✓		
	Suspense		536				✓
	Discount Received	536			✓		
	Suspense		536				✓
2	Fixtures & Fittings	470				✓	
	Disposal		470	✓			
3	Debtor		380				✓
	Creditor	380			✓		
	Creditor	470					
	Cash/Bank		470				
4	Stock (write off)		800				✓
	Cost of Sales	800			✓		
5	Debtors	1,575				✓	
	Sales		1,575	✓			
6	Suspense	10,000				✓	
	Purchases		10,000	✓			
7	Debtors	189				✓	
	Sales		189	✓			
8	Creditors	21				✓	
	Returns Out (Purchases)		21	✓			
9	Drawings	86					
	Cash Sales		86	✓			

			£
Original Net Profit per draft accounts			41,004
Add			
Disposal (Cash Receipt)	(2)	470	
Sales (understated)	(5)	1,575	
Purchases (overstated)	(6)	10,000	
Sales (understated)	(7)	189	
Returns Out (Credit Note)	(8)	21	
Cash Sales (understated)	(9)	86	
		12,341	
Less			
Discount Allowed (understated expense)	(1)	536	
Discount Received (overstated income)	(1)	536	
Cost of Sales (Stock write off)	(4)	800	
Net Increase			10,469
Amended Net Profit			51,473

			£
Original Capital Employed per Accounts			352,600
Add			
Fixtures & Fittings (understated)	(2)	470	
Creditors (overstated)	(3)	380	
Debtors (understated)	(5)	1,575	
Suspense A/c	(6)	10,000	
Debtors (understated)	(7)	189	
Creditors (overstated)	(8)	21	
		12,635	
Less			
Suspense (Discount Allowed)	(1)	536	
Suspense (Discount Received)	(1)	536	
Debtors (overstated)	(3)	380	
Stock (write off)	(4)	800	
		2,252	
Net Increase			10,383
Revised Capital Employed			362,983

(b) $\dfrac{\text{Profit}}{\text{Capital Employed}} \times \dfrac{100}{1}$

$= \dfrac{51,473}{362,983} \times \dfrac{100}{1}$

$= 14.18\%$

Bonus = (14.18% – 10.00%) + 4.18%. Bonus only paid on complete percentages over 10% ∴ 4 x £300 = £1,200.

(c)   **Suspense Account**

	£Dr		£Cr
Cost of Sales	10,000	Balance b/f	8,928
		Discount Received	536
		Discount Allowed	536
	10,000		10,000

This question was testing your knowledge regarding Errors which affect the Trial Balance and hence a Suspense Account, and those errors which do not. It further tested your knowledge and understanding of the effect on Profit and on the Balance Sheet (Capital Employed). Finally, you were required to use the information you obtained to calculate a Return on Capital Employed in part (b) in order to determine the bonus.

ANSWER 26

This question is a test of ability to prepare accounts and final accounts from incomplete records.

Purchase daybook

Date		Total	Repair materials	Tools and equipment	Appliances for resale
1985		£	£	£	£
January	Dee & Co.	337.74		337.74	
	AB Supplies	528.20	528.20		
February	Simpson	141.34	141.34		
	Cotton Ltd.	427.40			427.40
	Dee & Co.	146.82	146.82		
March	AB Supplies	643.43	643.43		
	Simpson	95.60	95.60		
		£2,320.53	1,555.39	337.74	427.40

Sales daybook

Date		Total	Repair work	Appliance sales
1985		£	£	£
January	D. Hopkins	362.80	362.80	
	P. Bolton	417.10	417.10	
February	G. Leivers	55.00		55.00
	M. Whitehead	151.72	151.72	
	N. John Ltd.	49.14		49.14
	A. Linneker	12.53		12.53
March	E. Horton	462.21	462.21	
	S. Ward	431.08	431.08	
	W. Scothern & Co.	319.12	319.12	
	N. Annable	85.41	85.41	
		£2,346.11	2,229.44	116.67

Cash Book (debit side)
Receipts

Date	Item	Discount allowed £	Total £	Debtors £	Repair work £	Appliance Sales £	Sundries £
1985							
Jan.	Capital		250.00				250.00
	Loan		2,000.00				2,000.00
	Repairs		69.44		69.44		
Feb.	D. Hopkins	5.80	357.00	357.00			
	Repairs		256.86		256.86		
Mar.	P. Bolton		417.10	417.10			
	G. Leivers		55.00	55.00			
	A. Linneker		12.53	12.53			
	S. Ward	5.08	426.00	426.00			
	Repairs		182.90		182.90		
	Appliances		112.81			112.81	
		£10.88	4,139.64	1,267.63	509.20	112.81	2,250.00

Cash book (credit side)
Payments

Date	Item	Discount received £	Total £	Creditors £	Repair materials £	Drawings and bank £	Expenses £
1985							
Jan.	Repair materials		195.29		195.29		
	Rent		400.00				400.00
	Rates		150.00				150.00
	Stationery		32.70				32.70
	Car expenses		92.26				92.26
	Drawings		160.00			160.00	
Feb.	Repair materials		161.03		161.03		
	Sundries		51.54				51.54
	Car expenses		81.42				81.42
	Drawings		160.00			160.00	
Mar.	Dee & Co.	7.74	330.00	330.00			
	AB Supplies		528.20	528.20			
	Simpson	3.34	138.00	138.00			
	Cotton Ltd.		130.00	130.00			
	Dee & Co.	6.82	140.00	140.00			
	Repair materials		22.06		22.06		
	Sundries		24.61				24.61
	Car expenses		104.52				104.52
	Drawings		160.00			160.00	
	Bank		500.00			500.00	
	Balance c/f		578.01				
		£17.90	4,139.64	1,266.20	378.38	980.00	937.05

Creditors Ledger Control

1985		£Dr	1985		£Cr
March	Cash paid	1,266.20	*March*	Purchases	2,320.53
	Discount received	17.90			
	Balance c/f	1,036.43			
		£2,320.53			£2,320.53
			April	Balance b/f	£1,036.43

Debtors Ledger Control

1985		£Dr	1985		£Cr
March	Sales	2,346.11	*March*	Cash received	1,267.63
				Discount allowed	10.88
				Balance c/f	1,067.60
		£2,346.11			£2,346.11
April	Balance b/f	£1,067.60			

Sales

1985		Repairs £	Appliances £	1985		Repairs £	Appliances £
March	Trading account	2,738.64	229.48	March	Debtors ledger control	2,229.44	116.67
					Cash received	509.20	112.81
		£2,738.64	£229.48			£2,738.64	£229.48

Cost of sales

1985		Repairs £	Appliances £	1985		Repairs £	Appliances £
March	Creditors ledger control	1,555.39	427.40	March	Stock c/f	691.02	320.58
	Cash paid	378.38			Trading account	1,242.75	106.82
		£1,933.77	£427.40			£1,933.77	£427.40

M. Faraday
Trading and profit and loss account
for the quarter ended 31 March 1985

	Repairs £	Appliances £	Total £
Sales	2,738.64	229.48	2,968.12
Cost of sales	1,242.75	106.82	1,349.57
Gross profit	1,495.89	122.66	1,618.55

Add Non-Trading Income		
Discount received		17.90
Less Expenses		1,636.45
Less Expenses		
Discount allowed	10.88	
Car expenses	278.20	
Rent (400.00—200.00 prepaid)	200.00	
Rates	150.00	
Heating and lighting	265.00	
Stationery	32.70	
Sundry expenses	76.15	
Loan interest (10% x £2,000 x 3/12)	50.00	
Depreciation		
: car	100.00	
tools and equipment (339.74—300.00)	37.74	
		1,200.67
Net profit		£435.78

M. Faraday
Balance sheet as at 31 March 1985

	Cost £	Provision for Depreciation £	Net £
Fixed assets			
Tools and equipment	337.74	37.74	300.00
Car	700.00	100.00	600.00
	£1,037.74	137.74	900.00
Current assets			
Stocks: repair materials	691.02		
appliances	320.58		
		1,011.60	
Debtors		1,067.60	
Prepayments		200.00	
Bank		500.00	
Cash		578.01	
		3,357.21	
Less			
Current liabilities			
Creditors	1,036.43		
Accruals			
(£50 interest plus £265 heating)	315.00		
		(1,351.43)	
Working capital or Net Current Assets			2,005.78
Net assets employed			£2,905.78
Financed by			
Capital: opening (£700 + £250)		950.00	
Add: net profit for quarter		435.78	
		1,385.78	
Less: drawings		(480.00)	
Long term liabilities:			905.78
10% loan (unsecured)			2,000.00
Capital employed			£2,905.78

ANSWER 27

This is a test of ability to produce absolute figures from a given set of relationships in ratio form.

M. Smith
Forecast trading and profit and loss account
for year ended 31 December 1986

	£	£
Sales (100/(100–28) x Cost of sales)		140,000
Opening stock	20,000	
Add Purchases	97,800	
	117,800	
Less Closing stock ((18,500 x 2) – 20,000)	(17,000)	
Cost of sales is therefore		100,800
Gross profit (28% x sales)		39,200
Expenses are therefore		(25,200)
Net profit for the year (10% x sales £140,000)		£14,000

M. Smith — Forecast Balance Sheet
as at 31st December 1986

Fixed Assets	£ Cost	£ Provision for Depreciation	£ Net Book Value
Fixed Assets (not specified)			
1.5 £50,000 net assets employed			
1.5 + 1.0	—	—	30,000
Current Assets			
Stocks (per trading a/c)	17,000		
Debtors (140,000 x 36.5/365)	14,000		
Bank	5,000	36,000	
Less Current Liabilities			
Creditors 97800 x 58.4	15,650		
365			
Accruals	350	(16,000)	
Net Current Assets or Working Capital			20,000
Total Net Assets			50,000
Financed by:			
Capital: opening at 1.1.86		40,000	
Add: net profit for year		14,000	
		54,000	
Less: drawings		(10,000)	
: closing at 31.12.86			44,000
Long term loan			6,000
Capital Employed			50,000

ANSWER 28

(a)

Gillespie
Claim for loss of stock destroyed by fire
on 25 August 1984

	£	£
Stock at cost, 30 June 1984		7,200
Purchases for the eight weeks to 25 August 1984		2,560
		9,760
Sales for the eight weeks to 25 August 1984	6,240	
Gross profit: $\frac{30}{130}$ x £6,240	1,440	
Cost price of sales		4,800
Total claim for loss of stock		4,960

(15 marks)   *(15 marks)*

(b)

Gillespie Profit and Loss Account
for the eight weeks ended 25 August 1984

	£	£
Sales		6,240
Less: Cost of goods sold		
Opening stock	7,200	
Purchases	2,560	
	9,760	
Less: Closing stock	4,960	
		4,800
Gross profit		1,440
Less: Expenses		
Wages	192	
Expenses	520	
Loss re under-insurance of fixtures and fittings	100	
		812
Net profit		628

Gillespie Balance Sheet on 25 August 1984

	£	£
CURRENT ASSETS		
Debtor — Insurance claim		7,660
Balance at bank		4,008
Cash in hand		120
		11,788
Current liabilities		
Trade creditors	1,120	
Expense creditors	280	
NET CURRENT ASSETS		1,400
		10,388
Representing:		
Proprietor's interest		
Capital account		9,000
Current account		
At 30.6.84	1,000	
Profit for period	628	
	1,628	
Less: Drawings	240	
Current Account at 25.8.84		1,388
CAPITAL EMPLOYED		10,388

(15 marks)

WORKINGS for part (a)

Gillespie
Combined cash and bank summary
for the period 1 July 1984 to 25 August 1984

	£ Cash	£ Bank		£ Cash	£ Bank
Balances b/f	80	1,960	Creditors for goods		
Cash banked		5,768	supplied		2,800
Cash sales	6,240		Expenses		920
			Wages (8 x £24)	192	
			Drawings (8 x £30)	240	
			Cash banked	5,768	
			Balances c/f	120	4,008
	6,320	7,728		6,320	7,728

Trade creditors

	£		£
Bank	2,800	Balances b/f	1,360
Balances c/f	1,120	Purchases	2,560
	3,920		3,920

Expense creditors

	£		£
Bank	920	Balance b/f	680
Balance c/f	280	Expenses	520
	1,200		1,200

ANSWER 29

1. **RICKY — Opening Statement of Affairs i.e. Balance Sheet at 1.1.85.**

	£ Cost	£ Provision for Depreciation	£ NBV
Fixed Assets			
Premises			15,000
Motor Vehicle			5,000
			20,000
Current Assets			
Stock	5,250		
Debtors	4,950		
Bank	3,200		
Cash	500		
	13,900		
Less Current Liabilities			
Creditors	4,850		
Accruals (Subs)	20		
	(4,870)		
Net Current Assets			9,030
Total Net Assets			29,030
Financed By			
Capital			29,030
Capital Employed			29,030

RICKY — Trading, Profit and Loss A/c
year ending 31.12.85

		£	£
	Sales (3)		72,650
	+ Cash Sales		150
			72,800
	Less Cost of Sales		
	Opening Stock	5,250	
	Add Purchases	38,015	
		43,265	
	Less Closing Stock	(4,375)	
	Cost of Goods Sold		(38,890)
	Gross Profit		33,910
	Less Expenses		
	Wages	3,120	
	Rates	1,200	
A	Light & Heat (900 + 300)	1,200	
	Advertising	2,250	
P	Postage & Stationery		
	(750 – 49)	701	
	Subscription	20	
	Road Tax	85	
	Insurance	120	
A	Petrol (M.V. running)		
	(720 + 240A)	960	
	Depreciation		
	Premises	300	
	Motor Vehicle	1,000	
		1,300	
	Total Expenses		(10,956)
	Net Profit		22,954

RICKY — Balance Sheet at 31.12.85

	£	£	£
	Cost	Provision for Depreciation	NBV
Fixed Assets			
Premises	15,000	300	14,700
Motor Vehicle	5,000	1,000	4,000
	20,000	1,300	18,700
Current Assets			
Stock	4,375		
Debtors	5,260		
Prepayments	49		
Bank	24,225		
Cash	500		
		34,409	
Less Current Liabilities			
Creditors	5,315		
Accruals	560		
		(5,875)	
		Net Current Assets	28,574
		Total Net Assets	47,234
Financed By			
Capital a 1.1	29,030		
Add Profit	22,954		
	51,984		
Less Drawings		(4,750)	
		Capital Employed	47,234

2. **Bank and Cash Control Accounts**

	£Dr				**£Cr**	
Receipts	Bank	Cash	Payments		Bank	Cash
1.1 Balance b/f	3,200	500	Creditors		37,550	
Debtors	72,340		Wages (52 x 60)		3,120	
Cash Sales ¢		150	Rates		1,200	
			Light & Heat		900	
			Advertising		2,250	
			Postage & Stationery		750	
			Subscription '84		20	
			Road Tax		85	
			Insurance		120	
			Drawings		4,600	
			Petrol		720	
			Drawings	¢		150
			Balance c/f		24,225	500
	75,540	650			75,540	650

3. **Control Account for Debtors and Creditors**

Debtors Control a/c

	£Dr			**£Cr**
Balance b/f	4,950		Bank	72,340
Sales	72,650	31.12.85	Balance c/f	5,260
	77,600			77,600

4. **Creditors Control A/c**

		£Dr			**£Cr**
	Bank	37,550	1.1	Balance b/f	4,850
				Purchases	38,015
31.12.85	Balance c/f	5,315			
		42,865			42,865

ANSWER 30

V. BINGHAM — Cash and Bank Summary
for the year ended 31.10.81

	£Dr			£Cr	
	Bank	Cash		Bank	Cash
CAPITAL	18,600		Fixtures & Fittings	8,005	
			Vehicles	4,000	
CASH (Sales) ¢	86,800		Stationery & Advertising	1,488	
			Drawings	930	
DEBTORS	18,178		Electricity	521	
			Purchases (Creditors)	92,008	
CASH SALES		95,918	Staff Wages	8,184	
			Rent & Rates	2,108	
			Insurance	620	
			Legal Costs	645	
			Drawings		5,720
			Sundry Expenses		496
			Purchases		248
			Staff Wages & Insurance		2,654
			Bank ¢		86,800
			Balances c/f	5,069	—
	123,578	95,918		123,578	95,918

(1) Cash Sales must comprise £86,800 banked plus the items he took immediately out of cash for Drawings, Sundry Expenses, Purchases and Staff Wages.

(2) Next you need to prepare Control Accounts for Debtors to obtain the Sales figure and for Creditors to obtain Purchases.

Debtor Control A/c

	£Dr		£Cr
Balance b/f	NIL	Bank	18,178
Sales	20,732	Balance c/f	2,554
	20,732		20,732

Sales made on Credit terms	20,732
Sales made for Cash	95,918
Total Sales	116,650

Creditor Control A/c

	£		£
Bank	92,008	Balance b/f	NIL
Balance c/f	5,456	Purchases	97,464
	97,464		97,464

Purchases made on Credit terms	97,464
Add Cash Purchases	248
Total Purchases	97,712

(3) Goods £960 taken for Bingham's own use are classified as Drawings. They must not be included in his business purchases. The accounting entries are:

```
DR — DRAWINGS A/c          960
CR — PURCHASES A/c                    960
```

The effect is that Purchases (97,712 – 960) = 96,752 and Drawings (930 + 5,720 + 960) = 7,610

(4) Depreciation is to be charged thus:
Fixtures & Fittings   8,005 x 20% = 1,601
Vehicles   4,000 x 20% = 800

Note: I have not classified legal costs as capital expenditure because it does not say what the costs are in respect of. I have treated them as revenue. However, if legal costs were in respect of acquiring premises then it would be right and proper to treat them as capital expenditure.

V. BINGHAM — Trading, Profit and Loss A/c
for the year ended 31.10.1981

	£	£
Sales		116,650
Less Cost of Sales		
Opening Stock	NIL	
Add Purchases	96,752	
	96,752	
Less Closing Stock	(9,920)	
Cost of Goods Sold		(86,832)
Gross Profit		29,818
Less Expenses		
Stationery & Advertising	1,488	
Electricity (521 + 136A)	657	
Staff Wages & Insurance	10,838	
Rent & Rates (2,108 – 164P)	1,944	
Insurance (620 – 10P)	610	
Legal Costs	645	
Sundry Expenses	496	
Depreciation:		
Fixtures & Fittings	1,601	
Vehicles	800	
TOTAL EXPENSES		(19,079)
NET PROFIT		10,739

V. BINGHAM — Balance Sheet as at 31.10.1981

	£	£ Provision for	£ Net Book
Fixed Assets	Cost	Depreciation	Value
Fixtures & Fittings	8,005	1,601	6,404
Vehicles	4,000	800	3,200
	12,005	2,401	9,604
Current Assets			
Stock	9,920		
Debtors	2,554		
Prepayments	174		
Bank	5,069		
Cash	—		
		17,717	
Less Current Liabilities			
Creditors	5,456		
Accruals	136		
		(5,592)	
Net Current Assets - Working Capital			12,125
Total Net Assets			21,729
Financed by			
Capital (Introduced by Bingham)		18,600	
Add Retained Net Profit		10,739	
		29,339	
Less Drawings		(7,610)	
CAPITAL EMPLOYED			21,729

ANSWER 31

WORKING PAPER:
DAVID DENTON — Cash and Bank Summary
to 31st December

Receipts	£Dr	Payments	£Cr
Capital	6,500	Drawings (52 x £90)	4,680
Loan — Aunt Jane	4,000	Drawings — Travel Agent	280
Debtors — Sales	25,613	Rent in Advance	300
Cash — Sales	3,418	Lease — Premises	6,500
		Salary	3,000
		Fixed Assets — Plumbing Equip.	4,800
		Electricity to 30/9	1,122
		Motor Expenses	912
		General Expenses	1,349
			295
		Insurance	800
		Purchases	8,886
		Drawings — Cash	400
		Balance c/f	6,207
	39,531		39,531

Creditors Control A/c

	£Dr		£Cr
Bank a/c	8,886	Balance b/f	0
Balance c/f	714	Purchases	9,600
	9,600		9,600

to obtain purchases figure

Debtors Control A/c

	£Dr		£Cr
Balance b/f	0	Cash a/c	25,613
Sales a/c	29,863	Balance c/f	250
	29,863		29,863

to obtain Credit Sales
Note: Cash Sales are shown in the
Cash and Bank Summary

Accruals need to be made for:—

	£
Interest Owing	300
Accountants Fee	250
Rates Owing	135
Electricity Owing	374
	1,059

DAVID DENTON — Trading and Profit & Loss Account for the year ended 31.12.

	£	£
Sales — Credit		29,863
— Cash		3,418
		33,281
Less Cost of Sales		
Opening Stock	0	
Add Purchases	9,600	
	9,600	
Less Closing Stock	(580)	
Cost of Goods Sold		(9,020)
GROSS PROFIT		24,261
Less Expenses		
Secretarial Salary	3,000	
Rent (9/12 x 300 for this period) (P)	225	
Rates (9/12 x 180) (A)	135	
Electricity (3/12 x 1122 = 374 + 1122) (A)	1,496	
Insurance (9/12 x 800) (A)	600	
Motor Expenses	912	
General Expenses (1349 + 123)	1,644	
Loan Interest (10% x 4000 x 9/12) (A)	300	
Provision for Bad Debts	425	
Accountants Fee (A)	250	
Amortization of Lease (6500 x 10% x 9/12)	487	
Depreciation:		
Equipment (4800 x 20%)	960	
Vehicle (3600 x 25%)	900	
TOTAL EXPENSES		(11,334)
NET PROFIT		12,927

(A) = Accruals
(P) = Prepayments

DAVID DENTON — Balance Sheet at 31.12.

Fixed Assets	£ Cost	£ Provision for Depreciation	£ Net Book Value
Lease	6,500	487	6,013
Equipment	4,800	960	3,840
Vehicles	3,600	900	2,700
	14,900	2,347	12,553

Current Assets

Stock	580		
Debtors 4,250			
Less Provision for Bad Debts (425)	3,825		
Prepayments	275		
Bank *	6,084		
Cash *	123		
		10,887	

Less Current Liabilities

Creditors	714		
Accruals	1,059		
		(1,773)	
Net Current Assets			9,114
Total Net Assets			21,667

Financed by

Capital	10,100		
Add Net Profit	12,927		
	23,027		
Less Drawings	(5,360)		
Add Loan		4,000	
Capital Employed			21,667

*Note: In my Cash and Bank Summary I combined these figures to give a balance c/f £6,207.

ANSWER 32

1. LIFO

	ISSUES	£	REMAINING STOCK	£
Total issues = 50 units —	20 @ £32 =	640		
	10 @ £30 =	300		
	15 @ £25 =	375		
	5 @ £20 =	100	15 @ £20 =	300
		1415		300

FIFO	ISSUES	£	REMAINING STOCK	£
50 units —	20 @ £20 =	400		
	15 @ £25 =	375		
	10 @ £30 =	300		
	5 @ £32 =	160	15 @ £32 =	480
		1235		480

CALCULATION OF AVERAGES (AVCO)

16 June

UNIT	£	
20 @ £20	£400	Average Cost =
15 @ £25	£375	$\frac{775}{35}$ = £22.14
35	£775	

12 Sept.

UNITS	£	
19 @ £22.14	£420.66	Average Cost =
10 @ £30	£300	$\frac{720.66}{29}$ = £24.85
29	£720.66	

22 Dec.

UNITS	£	
17 @ £24.85	£422.45	Average Cost =
20 @ £32	£640	$\frac{1062.45}{37}$ = £28.71
37	£1062.45	

TRADING ACCOUNT for JERRY MANDA
for LIFO, FIFO, AVCO

	LIFO			FIFO		AVCO
	£	£	£	£	£	£
Sales		1600		1600		1600
Less Cost of Sales						
Opening stock	400		400		400	
Add Purchases	1315		1315		1315	
	1715		1715		1715	
Less Closing Stock	300		480		430.60	
		1415		1235		1284.40
GROSS PROFIT		185		£365		£315.60

2.   First In First Out gives the highest profit since older (lower) valued items are issued to cost of sales first. The last in First Out method yields the lowest profit because higher (latest) values are issued to cost of sales first. The Average Cost Method gives a profit somewhere between FIFO and LIFO because issue prices are smoothed.

ANSWER 33

(a) Redrafted balance sheet in a presentable form to obtain the figures needed:

Flaker Airfreight Balance Sheet at 30.6

	1984		1983	
	£	£	£	£
Balance sheet				
Fixed assets:				
Premises		250,000		150,000
Plant		260,000		140,000
		510,000		290,000
Current assets:				
Stocks	240,000		200,000	
Debtors	160,000		120,000	
	400,000		320,000	
Less Current liabilities:				
Creditors	90,000		60,000	
Overdraft	30,000		10,000	
	120,000		70,000	
Net Current Assets		280,000		250,000
Total Net Assets		790,000		540,000

(4 marks)

(b)

The Flaker Airfreight
Statement of source and application of funds
for the year ended 30 June 1984

	£	£
Source of funds		
Net profit before taxation		100,000
Adjustment for items not involving		
the movement of funds:		
Depreciation		50,000
Total generated from operations		150,000
Funds from other sources		
New capital introduced (W1)		150,000
		300,000
Application of funds		
Freehold premises purchased (W2)	100,000	
Plant and machinery purchased (W2)	170,000	
		270,000
		30,000
Increase in working capital		
Increase in stocks	40,000	
Increase in debtors	40,000	
(Increase) in creditors	(30,000)	
	50,000	
Movement in net liquid funds:		
Increase in bank overdraft	(20,000)	
		30,000

(16 marks)

(c) Workings

	£
1. Capital account at 30 June 1984	690,000
Capital account at 30 June 1983	440,000
	250,000
Less: Net profit for the year	100,000
New capital introduced	150,000

2. Fixed assets
Few details of fixed assets are given and therefore it is not possible to put into the statement anything other than a net movement on fixed assets, i.e. assume no disposals of fixed assets.

Then purchase of premises = £250,000 — 150,000
= £100,000

and purchases of plant and machinery
= £420,000 — £250,000
= £170,000

(4 marks)

(d) Comments on the change in working capital. An opportunity here for good students to mention ratios, e.g. Current Ratio, Acid Test.

(6 marks)

ANSWER 34

(a)   **Cash Budget for 3 months to 30.6.84**

Receipts		April	May	June
Balance b/f		1500	2710	2260
Income from Sales		5000	3500	4500
	(1)	6500	6210	6760

Payments				
Creditors		2000	2500	1500
Wages		800	700	900
Advertising		750	500	500
Repairs		90	100	80
Secretarial		150	150	150
	(2)	3790	3950	3130
Balance c/f (1) — (2)		2710	2260	3630

(b)   **Forecast Profit and Loss Statement
for 3 months to 30.6.84**

	April	May	June	Total
Sales	3500	4500	5500	13500
Less Cost of Sales (1)	1750	2250	2750	6750
Gross Profit (50%)	1750	2250	2750	6750
Less Expenses				
Wages	700	900	800	2400
Advertising	750	500	500	1750
Repairs	90	100	80	270
Secretarial	150	150	150	450
Depreciation (2)	167	167	167	501
	1857	1817	1697	5371
Net Profit	(107)	433	1053	1379

(c) Students should discuss the accrual concept briefly to illustrate why cash is not the same thing as profit.

ANSWER 35

A. Kennedy — Cash Budget for 3 months to 31.3

	Jan.	Feb.	March
Receipts			
Balances b/f	6000	4300	2600
Sales	—	3000	2000
Other	—	—	—
(1) TOTAL	6000	7300	4600
Payments			
Creditors		3000	2000
Rent	100	100	100
Wages	200	200	200
General Expenses	200	200	200
Machine Investment	1200	1200	1200
(2) TOTAL PAYMENTS	1700	4700	3700
Balance c/f (1) — (2)	4300	2600	900

Budgeted Profit Statement for 3 months to 31.3

	Jan.	Feb.	Mar.	TOTAL
Sales	3000	2000	5000	10000
Less Cost of Sales	1500	1000	2500	5000
GROSS PROFIT	1500	1000	2500	5000
Less Expenses				
Wages	200	200	200	600
Rent	100	100	100	300
General	200	200	200	600
Depreciation	75	75	75	225
TOTAL EXPENSES	575	575	575	1725
NET PROFIT	925	425	1925	3275

Cash & Profit Reconciliation Statement at 31.3   £

    Balance per Cash Budget   900

Non Cash Items in the Budgeted Profit Statement

    ADD March Sales   <u>5000</u>

Less Closing Stock	3000	
Depreciation	225	(3225)
		2675

Cash Items not appearing in Budget Profit Statement
i.e. Balance Sheet Items

Less Cash Balance 31/1	<u>6000</u>
	(3325)
Add Creditors for March purchases	3000
Machine Purchase Fixed Asset	3600
Balance per Budgeted Profit Statement	3275

A. Kennedy — Balance Sheet at 31.3

	£Cost	£Depn	£NBV
Fixed Assets			
Machine	3600	225	3375

Current Assets

Stock	3000	
Debtors	5000	
Prepayments	—	
Cash	900	
	8900	

Less Current Liabilities

Creditors	3000	
Accruals	—	
	3000	

N.C.A. — Working Capital		5900
Net Total Assets		9275

Financed By

Capital	6000	
Retained Profit	3275	
Capital Employed		9275

ANSWER 36

Mountfield Ltd. Cash Flow Forecast/Budget
for 3 months to 31.3.85

RECEIPTS	JAN.	FEB.	MAR.
Balance b/f	1,500	200	(1,300)
Debtors	3,100	4,000	5,000
Share issue	10,000		
L/Building Sale			15,000
	14,600	4,200	18,700
PAYMENTS			
Creditors	2,900	4,000	2,000
Tax			1,000
Dividend			1,000
Purchases P/Mach.	10,000		
Wages	1,000	1,000	1,000
G/Exps.	500	500	500
	14,400	5,500	5,500
Balance c/f (1) — (2)	200	(1,300)	13,200

Mountfield Ltd. Balance Sheet at 31.3.85

Fixed Assets	£ Cost	£ Depn.	£ N.B.V.
Land and buildings	40,000	4,250	35,750
Plant & machinery	10,000	250	9,750
Motor Vehicles	15,000	3,750	11,250
	65,000	8,250	56,750

Current Assets

Stock		3,500
Debtors 7,000		
140		
		6,860
Bank/Cash		13,200
		23,560

Less Current Liabilities

Creditors	2,000	
		2,000

Net Current Assets — Working Capital		21,560
Total Net Assets — Net Worth		78,310

Financed By

Share capital £1 ordinary shares	60,000	
Reserve	12,200	
	72,200	
Add Net Profit Retained	6,110	
Capital Employed		78,310

Sources and Application of Funds Statement
for the Year ending 31.3.85

Sources of Funds		£
1) Net profit before tax after charging depreciation		6,110
2) Add back items not involving the movement of funds (i.e. NON-CASH) Depn.		250
Total funds generated from operations (trading)		6,360

Funds from Other Sources		
3) Proceeds from share issue		10,000
Total funds from all sources		16,360

Application of Funds		
4) Taxation paid		1,000
5) Dividends paid		1,000
Working Capital		14,360

6) Decrease in stock	(2,000)		
7) Increase in debtors	3,760		
8) Decrease in Creditors	900		
		2,660	
9) Movement in Net Liquid Funds Change in Cash Balance		11,700	
			14,360

Working

$$\text{Mark Up} = \frac{\text{Gross Profit}}{\text{Cost of Sales}} = \frac{60}{100} \qquad \text{Margin} = \frac{\text{Gross Profit}}{\text{Sales}} = \frac{60}{100} \quad \frac{3}{8}$$

$$\frac{3}{5} \qquad\qquad \frac{3}{5+3} = \frac{3}{8}$$

DISPOSAL ACCOUNT

	£Dr		£Cr
L & B a cost	10,000	Cash	15,000
Profit	6,000	Depreciation Provision	1,000
	16,000		16,000

Mountfield Ltd. Budgeted Profit & Loss Account for 3 months to 31.3.1985

	£	£
Sales		16,000
Less Cost of Sales		
Opening Stock	5,500	
Add purchases	8,000	
	13,500	
Less Closing Stock (2)	3,500	
		10,000
Gross Profit		6,000
Add Non-Trading Income		
Profit on disposal		6,000
		12,000
Less Expenses		
Wages	3,000	
General Expenses	1,500	
Depreciation		
Land and Buildings 250		
Plant and Machinery 250		
Motor Vehicles 750		
	1,250	
Provision for Bad Debts	140	
		5,890
Net Profit		6,110

ANSWER 37

(1) 1983 Stock/Cost of Sales x 365 = No. of days in stock
10,000 / 20,000 x 365 = 182.5 days
1984 15,000 / 25,000 x 365 = 219 days
or
Av. Stock/Av. Cost of Sales x

365 = 202.77 days

This firm would appear to be holding far too much stock in view of current trading levels. The stock holding position has worsened since 1983.

(2) Debtors / Sales x 365 = No. of days in debtors
1983 5,000/30,000 x 365 = 60.8 days
1984 9,000/34,000 x 365 = 96.6 days
Average Debtors/Average Sales x 365
i.e. 1983
21,875 x 365 = 79.8 days

The time taken to collect debtors appears to have worsened from 1983 to 1984. Too much credit is being allowed to customers.

(3) Creditors /Purchases x 365 =
1983 6,000/22,000 x 365 = 99.5 days
1984 4,000/30,000 x 365 = 48.7 days
Av. 5,000/26,000 x 365 = 70.2 days

It would appear that the firm is paying its creditors much more promptly in 1984 and owing to the extended credit period being taken by debtors, may find itself in cash flow difficulties unless it tightens up on debtors and reduces stock levels.

(4)   The Working Capital Cycle:

                                     No. of Days

                           1983   1984   Av.
Stock   =   182.5   219   202
Debtors   =   61   97   80
                           _____   ___   ___
                           243.5   316   282
Creditors   =   99.5   49   70
                           _____   ___   ___
                           144   267   212
                           =====   ===   ===

The length of time in which the working capital turns
over has increased by (267 — 144) 123 days in 1984.

(5)   Net Profit/Capital Employed

                               1983   1984
                               %   %
       2,000   =   2.9   NIL
       ──────   ===   ===
       68,500

Maybe the shareholders ought to consider investing their
funds elsewhere to earn a higher rate of return.

(6)   Gross Profit/Sales   1983   1984

                               33.33%   26.47%
                               ======   ======

The Cost of Sales have risen sharply in 1984.

(7)   Net Profit/Sales   1983   1984

                               6.7%   NIL
       Expenses/Sales   1983   1984

                               26.6%   26.7%

Although expenses have risen from £8,000 to £9,100
they have remained constant in terms of sales value. The
reduced profitability has resulted from the higher costs of
stock used in sales.

(8) Acid Test Debtors + Cash/Current Liabilities
1983 = 5,500/7,000 = .78 : 1
1984 = 9,400/4,000 = 2.35 : 1

There are sufficient near liquid and liquid assets to meet current liabilities.
However, if you calculate the worsening length of time it takes for Debtors to turn into cash then the position above is not quite as good as it may appear to be in isolation.

1.(b) Working Capital is important because it is the lifeblood of the business. It needs to circulate quickly to drive the business forward. I would expect students to discuss this idea, explain what is meant by working capital and perhaps illustrate their comments by using some of the ratios they calculated in **(a)**.

1.(c) A reserve is an amount set aside for a specific reason and is not available for distribution to shareholders e.g. Profit and Loss Reserve.

ANSWER 38

This is a test of ability to calculate earnings, earnings per share and gearing.

Estimated profit and loss account
for year ended 31 December 1984

	X PLC		Company Y PLC		Z PLC	
	£000	£000	£000	£000	£000	£000
Profit before interest and tax		5,000		5,000		5,000
Interest		Nil		Nil		(400)
Profit before tax		5,000		5,000		4,600
Taxation (40%)		(2,000)		(2,000)		(1,840)
Profit after tax		3,000		3,000		2,760
Dividends						
: preference	Nil		(320)		(160)	
: ordinary (12%)	(720)		(480)		(120)	
		(720)		(800)		(280)
Profit for year retained		2,280		2,200		2,480

Estimated profit and loss accounts
for year ended 31 December 1984

	X PLC			Company Y PLC			Z PLC	
	£000	£000	£000		£000	£000		£000
(i) *Earnings:*								
Profit after tax		3,000			3,000			2,760
less Preference dividends		Nil			(320)			(160)
		3,000			2,680			2,600
Number of ordinary shares		8,000,000			16,000,000			4,000,000
Basic earnings per share		37.5p			16.75p			65.0p
(ii) *Gearing* (Preference capital plus debentures: ordinary shareholders' funds)		0:10			4:6 = 0.6:1			6:4 = 1.5:1
		Zero			Medium			High

Earnings per share moves roughly proportionate to changes in profit after tax in a low geared company but disproportionately in a high geared company.

ANSWER 39

ROCK — Trading, Profit & Loss Account
for the year to 31st August 1984

	T.V. £		Video £		Total £	
Sales						
Cash	180,000		—		180,000	
HP a Cash Prices	—		380,000		380,000	
HP a HP Prices	140,000		—		140,000	
HP Interest (note 1)	—		24,700		24,700	
		320,000		404,700		624,700
Less Cost of Sales:						
Opening Stocks	—		—		—	
Add Purchases	150,000		140,000		290,000	
	150,000		140,000		290,000	
Less Closing Stock	(7,500)		(7,000)		(14,500)	
Cost of Goods Sold		(142,500)		(133,000)		(275,500)
National Gross Profit & Interest	177,500					
Less Provision for Unrealized Profit (2)	(65,625)					(65,625)
Gross Profit	111,875		271,700		383,575	
Less Expenses						
Retailing			179,275			
Depreciation (20% Cost)			9,000			
Total Expenses						(188,275)
Net Profit						195,300

Notes:

	£
1. Video HP Interest — Total Sales HP	478,800
less total cash sales	
(380 x £100)	380,000
	98,800

Assuming Sales occur evenly throughout the year an average of the annual interest receivable should be included in the Trading Account for the year to 31st August 1984, i.e. £98,800 for two years = £49,400 for 1 year to average $\frac{49,400}{2}$ = 24,700

The provision therefore is £98,800 – 24,700 Interest due) = £74,100 not yet due.

2. Provision for unrealized profit on T.V.'s

	£
Total HP Selling Price (350 x £400) =	140,000
less Cost of Sales (350 x £400)	52,500
Total Gross Profit on HP Sales	87,500

Apportioned pro rata to cash collected

$$\text{Amount due} = \frac{£105,000 \text{ (HP Debtors)} \times £87,500}{140,000}$$

$$= £65,625$$

3. Retailing and Depreciation Expenses have not been apportioned to T.V. and Videos, since the question does not provide sufficient detail to do so.

ROCK — Balance Sheet at 31st August 1984

	£ Cost	£ Provision for Depreciation	£ N.B.V.
Fixed Assets	45,000	9,000	36,000
Current Assets			
Stocks		14,500	
Debtors		1,000	
HP Instalments (not yet due) T.V.	105,000		
Less Provision for Unrealized Profit	(65,625)	39,375	
HP Instalments (not yet due) Videos	342,000		
Less Provision for interest not yet due	(74,100)	267,900	
		322,775	
Less Current Liabilities			
Creditors	121,000		
Bank Overdraft	8,475		
		(129,475)	
Net Current Assets — Working Capital			193,300
Total Net Assets			229,300
Financed by			
Capital a 1.9.83	50,000		
Add Net Profit	195,300	245,300	
Less Drawings		(16,000)	
CAPITAL EMPLOYED			229,300

ANSWER 40

LENNON LIMITED
Working Paper

1. **COST OF SALES ADJUSTMENT**

Historic cost of sales	£80,000
Stock prices rose by	15%
Stock turnover	3 times per annum

$$C.O.S.A. = \frac{15\%}{3} \times 80,000 = \quad £4,000$$

Journal

	£ Dr	£ Cr
Cost of sales	4,000	
Current cost reserve		4,000

2. **REVALUATION OF STOCK**

Closing stock = £50,000

$$\text{Revalued stock} = £50,000 \times \frac{15\%}{3} = £2,500$$

Therefore, revalued stock = £52,500

Journal

	£ Dr	£ Cr
Stock	2,500	
Current cost reserve		2,500

3. **DEPRECIATION ADJUSTMENT**

	£ Historic	£ Current	£ Current Cost Adjustment
Cost	80,000	96,000	16,000
Depreciation	10,000	12,000	2,000
N.B.V.	70,000	84,000	14,000

Journals

	£ Dr	£ Cr
i) Depreciation Fixed Assets	2,000	
Current Cost Reserve		2,000
ii) Fixed Asset Cost	16,000	
Current Cost Reserve		16,000

4. MONETARY WORKING CAPITAL ADJUSTMENT

	£
Debtors	30,000
Creditors	20,000
	10,000

M.W.C.A. = 2% x 10,000 = £ 200

Journal

	£ Dr	£ Cr
Monetary Working Capital on C. Cost P/L	200	
Current Cost Reserve		200

5. GEARING ADJUSTMENT

Historical Cost Capital Employed	=	£160,000
Fixed Asset Revaluation	=	£ 14,000
Stock Revaluation	=	£ 2,500
Current Cost Capital Employed	=	£176,500

$$\text{Gearing Adjustment} = \frac{\text{Borrowed funds} - \text{Cash}}{\text{Current cost capital employed}} \times \frac{100}{1}$$

$$= \frac{£25,000 - £30,000}{£176,500} \times \frac{100}{1}$$

$$= \frac{-£5,000*}{£176,500} \times \frac{100}{1}$$

*This "top line" figure is negative, therefore a **gearing adjustment is not used.**

6. TOTAL CURRENT COST RESERVE

	£
Cost of sales adjustment	4,000
Stock revaluation	2,500
Fixed asset revaluation	14,000
Monetary working capital adjustment	200
Depreciation adjustment	2,000
Current cost reserve	22,700

LENNON LIMITED
Current Cost Operating Statement
for year ended 31.12.83.

	£	£
Historical cost operating profit (before interest and dividends)		50,000
Less current cost adjustments:		
Cost of sales adjustment	4,000	
Depreciation adjustment	2,000	
Monetary working capital adjustment	200	
		6,200
Current cost operating profit (before interest and dividends)		43,800
Less interest		2,500
Current cost operating profit (attributable to shareholders)		41,300
Less dividend		12,500
Retained profit		£28,800

LENNON LIMITED
Current Cost Balance Sheet
as at 31.12.83

	£	£	£
Fixed Assets	Cost	Depreciation	N.B.V.
	96,000	12,000	84,000
Current Assets			
Stock	52,500		
Debtors	30,000		
Cash	30,000		
		112,500	
Less Current Liabilities			
Creditors		20,000	
			92,500
			£176,500
Financed by:			
Share capital			100,000
Reserves (P/L)			28,800
Current cost reserve			22,700
Shareholders' funds			151,500
Debentures			25,000
			£176,500

ANSWER 41

S. SIMPSON — Bank Reconciliation Statement
as at 31 January 1984

	£	£
Balance per Cash Book at 31.1.84		203.35
Add:		
Adjustment for cash book error		
31 January Sales debited in cash book as		
£210.00 instead of £230.00		20.00
Adjusted cash book balance		223.35
Add:		
Unpresented cheques:		
Gray's Machines Ltd.	645.10	
P. Swann	124.64	
Wages	320.40	
		1,090.14
		1,313.49
Less:		
Bank lodgement not yet entered in		
bank statement	230.00	
Bank charges	15.40	
Standing order	12.00	
Standing order debited in error — now		
cancelled	44.00	
		301.40
Balance per bank statement a 31.1.84		£1,012.09

ANSWER 42

The first thing to do is write up the cash book (i.e. Bank Account in the Nominal Ledger) with those items shown on the Bank Statement but which are not already in the cash book.

BANK ACCOUNT — Nominal Ledger

	£Dr		£Cr
Balance b/f	3,600	Bank Charges	25
B.G.C. — Smith	100	Standing Order — Rent	25
		Direct Debits	50
		Balance c/f	3,600
	3,700		3,700

Now we can identify those items in the Cash Book but not on the Bank Statement and prepare a Reconciliation.

Bank Reconciliation Statement

	£
Balance per Cash Book	3,600
Add unpresented cheques:—	
Wages — Cheque 002	600
	4,200
Less Bank Lodgements not yet	
on Statement Parfitt	(750
Balance per Bank Statement	3,450

ANSWER 43

ADF LTD — Journal Entries

Date	Account Name	£Dr	£Cr
30.6	DISPOSAL ACCOUNT — FIXED ASSET MOTOR VEHICLES A/c (to transfer the disposed asset to a disposal a/c.)	7,000	7,000
30.6	PROVISION FOR DEPRECIATION A/c DISPOSAL ACCOUNT — (transfer the depreciation provision no longer required to the disposal a/c.)	4,000	4,000
30.6	BANK A/c DISPOSAL ACCOUNT (with proceeds from disposal).	5,100	5,100

M.V. Disposal Account

	£Dr		£Cr
M.V. Fixed Assets a/c	7,000	Provision for Depreciation a/c	4,000
Profit on Disposal	2,100	Bank a/c	5,100
	9,100		9,100

ANSWERS TO MULTIPLE CHOICE

44. The Going Concern Concept, Prudence or Conservation, Accruals or Matching Principle, Consistency.

45b, 46c, 47c, 48a, 49b, 50a, 51a, 52c, 53b, 54e, 55e, 56d 57e, 58d, 59a, 60d, 61d.

ANSWER 62

Break Even Point and Marginal Costing

(1)

	£	£
Estimated Selling Price		12
Less Variable Costs		
Direct Labour Costs	5	
Direct Materials	4	
		9
Contribution to Fixed Overheads		3

(2) Fixed Overheads are estimated to be — £1,500.
Therefore by using:

B/E Point = Fixed Overheads
Contribution per Unit

We have:

B/E Point = $\frac{1500}{3}$ = 500

Break Even Point Occurs at 500 units of Output.

(3)   **Budgeted Profit Statement for the year
at 550 units**

	£
Sales	6,600
Less	
Variable Costs	4,950
	1,650
Less	
Fixed Costs	1,500
PROFIT	150

(4) The Margin of Safety is:—

Estimated or Actual Output — Break Even Quantity

550 units — 500 units

= 50 units

The 'margin of safety' that the business has is 50 units.
This means it can afford to lose 50 contributions and still
manage to break-even.

(5) Before we can plot the points we need to know what they
are:

Output Quantity	Total Sales Revenue	Total Variable Cost	Total Contribution	Total Fixed Cost	Total Cost	Profit (Loss)
0	0	0	0	1,500	1,500	(1,500)
100	1,200	900	300	1,500	2,400	(1,200)
200	2,400	1,800	600	1,500	3,300	(900)
300	3,600	2,700	900	1,500	4,200	(600)
400	4,800	3,600	1,200	1,500	5,100	(300)
500	6,000	4,500	1,500	1,500	6,000	0
600	7,200	5,400	1,800	1,500	6,900	300
700	8,400	6,300	2,100	1,500	7,800	600
800	9,600	7,200	2,400	1,500	8,700	900
900	10,800	8,100	2,700	1,500	9,600	1,200
1000	12,000	9,000	3,000	1,500	10,500	1,500

Note:
The margin of safety represents the amount by which sales
output may fall without the firm incurring a loss.

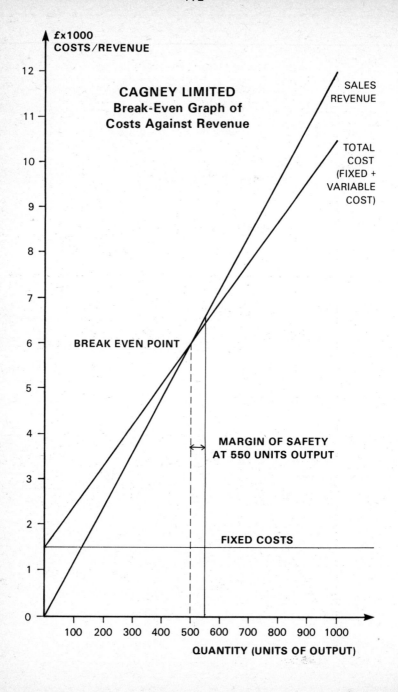

(6)

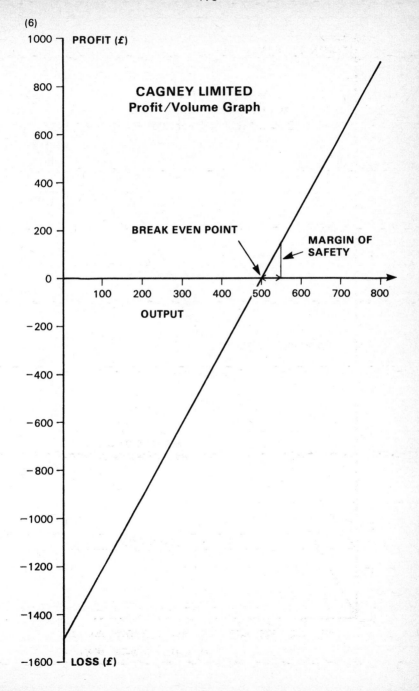

CAGNEY LIMITED
Profit/Volume Graph

(7) The Profit/Volume Ratio is really the Contribution/Sales Ratio.

Thus $\dfrac{£3}{£12} = 1:4$

or expressed as a percentage 25%.

For every £4 worth sold Cagney will make £1 contribution towards fixed overheads. Of course once those fixed overhead costs are covered, each £1 of contribution will indeed be profit.

ANSWER 63

JOURNALS	£Dr	£Cr
Note (2) Bad Debt Expense A/c	145	
Provision for Bad Debts A/c		145
(3) Depreciation Expense A/c Land & Buildings	1,440	
Provision for Depreciation L & B		1,440
Depreciation Expense A/c Motor Vehicle	1,406^{25}	
Provision for Depreciation — M.V.		1,406^{25}
(4) Prepayments A/c	200	
Rent and Rates Expense A/c		200
(5) Advertising Expense A/c	150	
Accruals A/c		150

Amended Trial Balance at 31.12.85

	£Dr	£Cr
Land & Buildings @ cost	72,000	
Motor Vehicles @ cost	10,000	
Stock a 1.1.85	6,250	
Debtors	5,150	
Bank	2,750	
Cash	100	
Purchases	19,650	
Drawings	7,000	
Carriage In	250	
Returns In	500	
Returns Out		350
Discount Received		600
Discount Allowed	450	
Wages & Salaries Exp.	2,500	
Postage & Stationery Exp.	250	
Rent & Rates Exp.	1,200	
Light & Heat Exp.	1,250	
Bad Debt Exp.	395	
Advertising Exp.	150	
Sales		34,500
Creditors		6,350
Capital		60,000
Loan		3,375
Accruals		150
Prepayment	200	
Depreciation Exp. (Land & Buildings)	1,440	
Depreciation Exp. (Motor Vehicles)	1,406.25	
Provision for Depreciation (L & B)		21,440
Provision for Depreciation (M.V.)		5,781.25
Provision for Bad Debts		345
	132,891.25	132,891.25

APPENDIX I

Summary of the Balance Sheet Equation

ASSETS + EXPENSES = CAPITAL + LIABILITIES + REVENUE		
INCREASE	DR	CR
REDUCE	CR	DR

FIXED ASSETS

Items of 'CAPITAL EXPENDITURE' which will generate income and be consumed over a number of financial periods (i.e. greater than one year).

e.g. Plant and Machinery
Land and Buildings
Motor Vehicles etc.

Their consumption is charged as an expense called DEPRECIATION.

CURRENT ASSETS

Items used in the present financial period to operate the business (consumed in less than one year).

e.g. STOCK
DEBTORS and PREPAYMENTS
BANK
CASH

EXPENSES

'Allocations' for non-trading goods and services consumed in the present financial period 'matched' with Revenue of the financial period.

e.g. Administration
Sales and Marketing
Factory Overheads
Finance Expenses (Bank Charges and Loan Interest etc.)

CAPITAL

The funds the owner puts into the business to finance it, i.e. Equity.

Sole Trader — Owner's Money
Partnership — Owners' Money
Private Ltd. — (Shareholders'
PLC (Money
Cooperatives/Clubs — Members' funds

N.B. DRAWINGS in the case of Sole Traders and Partnerships are the opposite of CAPITAL and treated as such. — Limited Companies, Private and Public both pay DIVIDENDS.

LIABILITIES

Purchases (from Suppliers for Trading Stock) bought on credit terms from CREDITORS not yet paid for. Or Expenses incurred but not yet paid. CURRENT (short term) Creditors which may be Trade or Expense, Accruals for expenses or goods. LONG TERM — Bank Loans, Mortgages, Debentures etc.

REVENUE

Trading Income from SALES or Non-Trading Income, e.g. Royalties, Discount Received, Commission Income, Patent Income or Income from the Disposal of Fixed Assets.

THE BASIC CONCEPTS SERIES

The Basic Concepts series attempts to explain in a clear and concise manner the main concepts involved in a subject. Paragraphs are numbered for ease of reference and key points are emboldened for clear identification, with self assessment questions at the end of each chapter. The texts should prove useful to students studying for A level, professional and first year degree courses. Other titles in the series include:—

QUESTIONS AND ANSWERS SERIES

These highly successful revision aids contain questions and answers based on actual examination questions and provide fully worked answers for each question. The books are written by experienced lecturers and examiners and will be useful for students preparing for O and A level, foundation and BTEC examinations. Subjects include:—

Economics by G. Walker
Accounting by T. Hines
Multiple Choice Economics by Dr. S. Kermally
O level Mathematics by R.H. Evans
A level Pure Mathematics and Statistics by R.H. Evans
A level Pure and Applied Mathematics by R.H. Evans
O level Physics by R.H. Evans
O level Chemistry by J. Sheen
O level Human Biology by D. Reese